Robert Baranyi
RICHER
WITHOUT
WASTE

Robert Baranyi
2018
All rights reserved!
Translation: Áron Nagy

ISBN: 978-615-00-1241-4

RICHER WITHOUT WASTE

How to live sustainable life

Robert Baranyi

2018.

Introduction

'Scientia potentia est' – 'Knowledge is power' – Sir Francis Bacon[1]

Many people do not even realize how much money they can save by reducing their costs and expenses, and even those who are aware of it often cannot decide how to begin. However, by reading this book, it is not so difficult, anyone can easily learn how to save money, i.e. how to be better-off living without waste.

When the news was released in the media why rich people, such as Steve Jobs, the founder of giant corporation Apple, or Facebook founder Mark Zuckerberg, as well as Tom Szaky[2], who is less familiar compared to them, were dressed in the same clothes every day, especially the latter went to work wearing the same outfit, everyone's eyes were on stalks.

Steve and Mark did so in order to avoid having to worry on a daily basis about what clothes to put on, as 'everyday thinking' consumes a lot of energy, taking time away from creative design, while dealing with waste recycling, Tom chose to ignore fashion trends not to produce unnecessary waste.

Of course, Tom Szaky did not get rich from ignoring fashion and buying fewer clothes, but he began to think differently about waste. His company, TerraCycle, bombed multinational companies with newer and newer ideas on how to recycle waste others had not attempted to do up until then, and after a while, these companies bought his ideas. Tom was on the up and up, although he did not do anything other than make money from stuff nobody needed anymore.

Although anyone can become a millionaire from waste, the purpose of this book is not to present business people like Tom, who have become quite rich owing to their revolutionary ideas in waste management, but rather to provide a recipe for average people about how to thicken their bank accounts by reducing waste at their workplaces, homes and other places, by saving energy or water, by using cheap or cheaper means of transport, by spending less on food yet eating properly and well while staying healthy; briefly, living well on little.

When reading these lines, many of you will raise the question spontaneously: 'How is it possible to live well on little?' For this, we need to acquire quite a lot of knowledge from this book, of which the most important piece is to understand what waste or rather the everyday waste production process is, what their synonyms are, and how we need to live to be able to economize a lot by producing less waste.

WHAT IS WASTE AND WASTE PRODUCTION?

If we are asked the question what waste is, many of us only think of the waste bin in our home, although waste is much more than that. It has its negative and positive aspects at the same time, however, obviously it is rather a negative thing, which, if we want to reduce or exclude it from our lives, teaches us to think wisely, which will positively influence our way of life, and change it fundamentally. Before replying the question of what waste really is in an entire book, we will ask six more questions in order to illustrate the widened concept of ordinary waste today in a consumer society:

If you do not use your smart phone, what will it produce? Waste? What is excess fat on obese people? Waste?

What is our piece of clothing stashed away unworn in the wardrobe for years? Waste?

When we pee in the shower, can we reduce waste and save the Earth?

In fact, what is the rubbish we scatter the sky with every day?

THE DIGITAL REVOLUTION

By the turn of the century it became clear that not only a millennium or the 20th century ended, but it was also the end of an era. The digital revolution is starting to play an increasingly important role in our lives, which has serious implications on our way of life and doing our job, thus our waste production. For instance, an IT professional or graphic designer, whose employer lives in the city, however they live close to the city, or work in the countryside, hardly keep contact with their bosses[3]. They do not need an office as before, and they do not need a car to commute to the city, and there is no need for a restaurant or bar to eat during the day, there is no need for a toilet to use, but they live and work at home, so they not only save a lot of money for the employer, but also for themselves.

How is it possible? It is enough to formulate three observations of the many.

Housing is much cheaper in the countryside, there are no high rents or property prices, and from the viewpoint of people working from the countryside, the expenses occurred from living in the city would be considered unnecessary expenses, ultimately waste.

Those who produce some of their foods themselves, typically they neither pay the price of production costs of fruit and vegetable growing, nor the trading profit, which would have to be paid in a city, constituting nothing more than unnecessary expenses that would be waste after all.

People living in rural areas, where living permanently in one place, they can do without a car, and if they still need to commute typically to a city, it is enough to ask for a car from a car-sharing portal - even without a driver in the future, a self-driving one - or they can use public transport, that means it is not necessary to buy a car and maintain it, which would result in unnecessary expenses, ultimately waste. Such people practically do not consume, the do not buy at supermarkets or just very little, so they do not produce as much waste as urban people do. If we really simplify the issue and presuppose earning equal salaries, rural people are able to save more money that their urban colleagues.

Actually, we will have more and more people like this, as an EU survey[4] has shown that half of the workers today would like to work from home, even on the condition that they would receive lower monthly wages compared to their present salary, a 20 percent reduced amount. It should naturally be added straight away that even if the survey did not assess how many percent of workers would move out from increasingly expensive cities to the countryside, it dealt with the number of people, who would like to work from home and statistically it demonstrates the trend that can be expected in the future.

However, not only those can live cheaper who move to the countryside as a consequence of the digital revolution, but those who settle certain living condition in the countryside, such as food production, while they continue living in the city, or those who consciously transform their daily living conditions as city dwellers, namely they properly manage their electricity, heating and water consumption. At the first reading, all this might seem difficult or even unbelievable, though there is no wizardry in it, and you will find more about it in the corresponding parts of the book.

WASTE IS A GLOBAL PROBLEM

Waste and waste production have become global problems today. For instance, New York[5] produces such large amounts of waste that the garbage mountains next to the city are almost visible form space. The megalopolis does not intend to compete with the Pyramids or the Great Wall of China, however, due to its waste production, it has 'caught up' with the world-famous buildings. I wonder what will once happen to the large amounts of waste. How will waste be neutralized? And what about the ever-expanding refills? No proper solutions have been found so far, however, hope is occasionally raised by some ideas. Just to give an example, due to the fact that Singapore[6] possesses little space for constructions, waste is incinerated, and an island is being built out of ashes, which serve as ground for mainly sea creatures and a mangrove forest. It is a temporary solution, as the ash island will once have to be neutralized in order not to pollute the environment. What will then happen to the wildlife settled there in the meantime?

Reading these lines, we cannot help but ask ourselves what can be done against the ever regenerating mountains of waste. The answer is simple. Besides the government, local authorities and companies entitled to deal with this problem; we ourselves can have a key role in doing against the accumulation of waste. Does it sound interesting? We may have our doubts or we may not understand.

Still it is so: we are also responsible for our waste production. According to statistical data, exclusively consumers can do about one third[5] of food waste production, as consumer society is about nothing else, but permanent and partly unnecessary shopping, whilst simultaneously keeping this example in mind, throwing one third of the food into trash.

HOW SHOULD WE START REDUCING WASTE? WHY IS IT WORTH DOING SO?

Well, not only unnecessary shopping should be given up, but we rather need to understand how waste production works in our living space, and how we can reduce it significantly.

According to our calculations, in the case of people becoming conscious in the meantime, monthly expenses of living style can be reduced by 30-40 percent, depending on how far you go with transforming your behavioral patterns, habits, i.e. changing your way of thinking. The basis of waste reduction is none other but the acquisition and continuous development of appropriate knowledge. Knowledge is power or the best investment, so we do not have to do anything just expediently use and utilize it.

LOTS OF GOOD IDEAS, LESS WASTE, MORE MONEY SAVED!

We might as well sum it up like this. Let's see how all this can be applied in practice.

NOTES:

1. https://en.wikipedia.org/wiki/Scientia_potentia_est

2. http://24.hu/elet-stilus/2015/04/05/egyetlen-nadragja-van-a-milliomos-magyar-sracnak/ -
https://en.wikipedia.org/wiki/Tom_Szaky

3. http://www.bbc.com/news/uk-england-norfolk-29552557?_ga=1.113905615.916690107.1
407856939

*4. http://hvg.hu/vallalat_vezeto/20160906_tavmunka_home_office_*

5. https://www.slideshare.net/ecovainc/ies-webinar-feeding-the-bottom-line-food-waste-101

6. http://www.nea.gov.sg/energy-waste/waste-management/semakau-landfill

Chapter 1 - What is waste?

'The best is waste not produced.'

INSTEAD OF DULL CONCEPTUAL DEFINITIONS

Cycle as a Pattern - Nature does not produce waste at all

School or university textbooks dealing with environmental protection and waste management use several conceptual determinations for waste.

Even if we find these books very useful, we will not follow them, but we will try to convey what waste is and how we can manage it at home by providing practical examples and a list of principles that can be attached to them instead. However, definitions will also be given where necessary. Let's take the first example, even if it is not primarily related to our household, but the operation of a company, as the example vividly demonstrates how we should approach the issue of waste that can be allied even in our home later.

Why is it worth for a company to produce without waste?

Before answering the question, we should consider a model. Nature has the property of not producing waste, to which perhaps the most beautiful example is a forest. In a forest, or biomass association, everything heads somewhere; every tiny building block has a role in the permanent and always restarting cycle. The leaves of trees fall at fall, out of which the destined organisms, especially fungi and bacteria produce humus, which will be utilized not only by trees, but by other plants, as trees will leaf again later in spring, so everything will restart from the beginning.

Here is a company which operates just like nature!

In his Ted lecture, architect Michael Pawlyn, holding the view of the cycle principle, spoke about an entrepreneurship, which practically excluded producing waste from its production. According to his narration, the Graham-Wilson company does not do more than buying cartons from some food manufacturers, which would otherwise be thrown away as waste, for example caviar distributor firms (Caviar Project out of carton)[1], and then after chopping the cartons, the company sells the product as litter for horses. When the horses have used it and got the litter 'soiled', it will be bought again and be given to worms or maggots as food, which may later become food for caviar spawning fish. As the result of abundant food, the fish can produce spawn again, which is further processed and the producers may deliver caviar to the shops, so the circle will be closed. More precisely, it will start again, while all waste is recycled.

There is no doubt that the company, which does not produce waste, can save a lot of costs, since a lot of expenses are consumed up by storing or neutralizing waste in the case of a company, as we referred to in the preface in connection with Tom Szaky.

However, this is not only true for companies, but, for instance, also for the operation of our households. We will write more about this in the respective chapters of the book. For the time being, it is enough to mention two everyday examples to properly illustrate that the majority of companies brush aside the cycle and create waste every day, although it could be otherwise. Of course, we will also talk about what we, ordinary people can do against the lavishness of companies.

Most of us take milk in cartons, and after consumption the cartons will be thrown into waste. Even if there are some known technologies by which beverage cartons can be recycled, we have to think over what would happen if we used a bottle at the same primary producer every time when we buy milk. Presumably we would get fresh (and real) milk at a cheaper price, while not polluting the environment with cartons, so more money would remain in our purse. Especially, when bearing in mind the maintenance of our health, we will learn to make kefir, yoghurt, different kinds of cheese, and other dairy products at home. Some dairy products like yoghurt are really beneficial for a healthy intestinal flora, which is the primary defense line of the entire immune system. In some remote Asian countries, where people live to the very ripe old age, the secret lies in their daily consumption of own-produced raw yoghurt.[2]

Nonetheless, it might be easier and more convenient to pop down to the shop and lift down the product from the shelf; however, in the meantime of doing so, we should always keep in mind how much extra money we pay for this, that would be unnecessary.

Having coffee produces huge mountains of waste

Having coffee and visiting the coffeehouse has been a popular for a long time. It would not be a problem in itself if it did not go hand in hand with producing mountains of waste recently, as our consumption habits seem to change related to having this black drink. The process is well-illustrated by this one-minute video[3], which has been uploaded on the Internet recently. We used to drink coffee from a cup, but nowadays this is not an 'accepted' way in our fast-paced world, coffee cups made of plastic have appeared instead, from which the bittersweet liquid can be drunk on the street or at our workplace.

According to the film, our changed habit leads into 58.000.000.000 waste glasses every year, thereby increasing our huge mountains of waste. What can we do against this? We can carry a cup with us or ask for one, so the plastic cup will become unnecessary, without any function, or we can select a coffeehouse in advance, where coffee is served in cups or mugs. But is there one like this at all?

With our proper approach and behavior, we can influence the market, and if it becomes a mass behavior, the chains will also consider whether the elimination of waste and re-adding the functions to ceramic cups, or the deployment of some technologies would be worth, e.g. for the production of plantable coffee cups[4], by which cups are degradable, and thus return to nature. However, all this is a longer process, and while it is cheaper to offer coffee in plastic cups than in degradable ones, companies will not switch to the latter solution.

This trend is clearly shown by the figures. In Great-Britain[5], 8 million cups are thrown into trash every day, which comes to approximately 3 billion annually, and only every 400th is recycled. However, legislative activity may curb this process. That is what happened in France, as not only the use of plastic cutlery and cups was banned, but the use of disposable plastic bags and tote bags as well. You can read more about this later, in the Housekeeping chapter.

So what can we do then?

It is not only worth considering what we can do for the environment, but we also have to consider how much we can save by not having our favorite drink in a coffeehouse, but at our workplace, or at home and we would take it with us. It is not only interesting because we can make it the way we like, but for other reasons as well. If you think about it, you can quickly calculate how much coffee you should drink at a coffeehouse to be worth making an investment into a coffee-maker (a long-lasting one, the production of which excludes the intention of planned obsolescence), which after some time would provide the possibility to have coffee for free compared to the quantity consumed at coffeehouses. Our calculations show that with the price of 30-40 coffees you can buy a mediocre, filter coffee-maker operating with ground coffee that is able to make even 5-10 cups of high-quality coffee at once. Can we economize with this? Obviously, yes.

If we are talking about saving, it really matters what kind of coffee-maker we use at home or at the workplace.

The terror of the coffee capsules

Naturally, a traditional coffee maker is apparently suitable for making ordinary coffee, unlike the more complicated machines, such as the fashionable capsule machines that appeared a few years ago, and which have started to spread all over the world. In addition, these expensive machines make coffee in various flavors, which have different names, give vent to spent capsule waste, which, of course, is not needed for the Earth and environment. Already in 2013, when the product appeared in mass production, more than 8 billion capsules were sold, enough to reach around the Equator ten times.

Unfortunately, only five percent of these widgets are made of recycled materials, the rest is nothing else, but a mountain of waste growing higher year by year. Of course, if people only bought simple coffee machines, there would be no need for the otherwise quite costly super machines using capsules, or the plastic widgets. The creators of the film Kill the K-Cup[6] also share this opinion, and uploaded a funny, yet thought-provoking video on YouTube. The two-minute spot shows that once all the capsules we have produced and used so far fall onto our heads and cause our death.

The video, although it does not go into details, may provoke further thoughts. We have to decide whether we need this super machine in our home or not. There is a coffee machine in every household, but if we buy the new machine, it becomes useless, a waste. The question is which one, because after a while we may get tired of the new machine and return to the old one, if we still have it.

This example shows that everything is decided in the mind, and we need to purchase and live according to a strict plan, never whimsically so that our home does not become a waste depot, while we do not wish to waste money unnecessarily to this or that. This of course does not mean we could not buy a newer or better machine to fulfil a function in our home if we want to. However, we should try to sell, give away or exchange the old one; this is not as bothersome as someone might think. We should try to find a new owner, otherwise it becomes waste. A home appliance not used is like money on a bank account, if it does not work, it does not make profit.

Hopefully, a time will come when coffee-drinking is not accompanied by building mountains of waste, however this is far, as chains are not concerned by this question yet. The news that Starbucks will get a rival as Nespresso also selling capsules will open a chain, the first coffeehouse in Vienna, then in London and other metropolises in the world, appeared in the beginning of 2015. This is not only because Nespresso wants to increase its profit this way, but other, smaller companies[7] started to appear and develop, companies, which have started to sell their own branded machines using capsules compatible with Nespresso. Would this be the end of the success of Starbucks?

So far it does not seem likely. The corporation makes its profit every year, and to achieve this, they use any solution which might increase their sales. Although it does not work and cannot work like a bank, yet they manage 1.2 billion USD only in their loyalty program[8], as all over the world 12 million members pay for their coffee with a loyalty card, probably at least once a day. Apparently, consumers save money by using this card, however, they do nothing else but increase the wealth of the company and decrease theirs. Would not it be cheaper if these consumers made their own coffee at home, and not produce waste consequently?

Of course, there are smart entrepreneurs, who see opportunity in waste, and also in the capsules. The American company TerraCycle[9], mentioned in the introduction, collects these capsules all over the world, so far 100 million. Their activities are heroic, yet it is only one drop in the ocean.

Planned obsolescence, planned waste

A bulb has been lighting in California, the garage of a fire department depot since 1901[10]. This might be interesting in itself, however not only this raises one's attention but also the fact that the performance of this bulb, which has been lighting continuously with small interruptions for over 100 years, over one million hours, also in the Guinness Book of Records, has been unmatched ever since. Why not? Because it is not worth to produce it, especially since 1920, when the concept of Planned Obsolescence[11] was invented, and this idea producing much profit was built into production cycles. Staying with the example above, today only those bulbs are designed and produced, which have an operation life of only 1000 hours. From these data one can easily calculate how many bulbs can be sold with planned obsolescence, and how many without it.

Critiques of Planned Obsolescence often refer to the example of the bulb, also the makers of the 2010 film, which, depicting the problem in detail was put on screen with the title The light bulb conspiracy[12]. The film starts with an interesting scene, when the service does not want to repair a printer, which can be repaired otherwise, for 110-120 EUR, as it is more worth to buy a new one for 39, which is quite strange when we consider the sums.

What are the conclusions?

We should not become victims of planned obsolescence. The consequences are double. If we want to have the printer repaired, we lose money, and not only once, as the machine designed with planned obsolescence in mind will break again, and we can waste money again on its repair. If we want to avoid this, we have to buy products, which were designed for lasting use, however this is not always easy, but nearly impossible in global capitalism struggling in the net of permanent economic growth.

If we manage to buy a printer, which survived the number of hours dictated by planned obsolescence for some reason, we can sit back. Or not?

When we shop, repair shops using their old, but good trick, put us in a dilemma. It also happened to us, when we wanted to have our four printer cartridges refilled. Although we had had the same cartridges refilled for years, and they knew us to some extent, a new colleague told us it might happen the cartridge cannot be refilled for some technical reason. Of course, he said this would not be a problem, if they cannot refill the cartridges for 4 dollars each, we can buy the new ones for 6. So we can decide to buy them now, and we do not have to wait 2-3 hours for the refill. When we answered firmly that we had not heard of any technical problem yet and we had had our cartridges filled there for years, the staff member was astonished and got red in the face, and stammered that they might be able to do this difficult job. However, we should consider how many decide to buy the new product, as they even gain time that they do not have to return for the new cartridges.

The story does not only teach us the lesson that we should not let ourselves be manipulated, but also to shop in a planned manner. We should not be deceived by advertisements, but take well-informed decisions. When we look around on the internet, or inquire in dedicated Facebook groups about the experiences on a given product, it soon becomes apparent whether it is worth spending our money on it, or not.

Therefore we should have our cartridges refilled again as long as we can, as it does not produce waste, and we will have more money in our purse. In this case, 8 dollars.

Unfortunately, we cannot always avoid buying a product, this was shown by the example of the printer or the cartridge, however, there are products, which can be produced on your own. No printers of course, but typically food, or everyday objects.

Self-sufficiency

Now, reading these lines we cannot even imagine how much food we can produce ourselves, either we live in the countryside and we have a little parcel of land, or if we live in the city, but we can produce part of our food supply, even a significant part of it, somewhere in the countryside, or as city-dwellers, we have an urban community garden.

This is really important, and not only because this way we produce little waste and can save a lot of money, but for other reasons as well. This is our health. Today it is a good project to stay healthy, not only because it is good to avoid painful diseases, but because we do not have to spend on the treatment of diseases and drugs. In addition, a person producing their own food can belong to a real community, and can be really happy.

In our welfare society the number of obese people is high, including children and young adults, and this has become a real global epidemic, there are many people suffering from diabetes, cancer, struggling after infarction or stroke, who become self-aware too late, and need permanent medical attention, although this should not be so in a health-conscious, well-bred society. The reasons are varied; one of them is outdated and unhealthy diet. Unfortunately, many buy unhealthy food in supermarkets and fast food restaurants, and consume these every day, every week. Thus they can get into a spiral, which can result in the so-called civilization diseases mentioned above. However, when someone starts to produce their own food and plan their weekly diet, and take their food to their workplace, can eat their own, cheaply produced food 24 hours a day, doing a lot for their health and weight.

How it is possible. It is enough to see the video[13], which shows how some young people left the treadmill of the city and started to produce their own vegetables and fruits, i.e. how they created their own agriculture. The recipe is given, anybody can do it, together with their friends and acquaintances. Community agriculture has many types all over the world, we do not even have to participate actively, only take over the delivery from the farmer employed by the community, usually in the city, for a given sum of money.

In the meantime, small farms can even be operated in the city, and some foods can be produced in urban community gardens. Such a community garden is the VICTORY GARDEN INITIATIVE[14] (VGI) in Milwaukee, which does not only operate an urban farm, but also organize various programs. They create high beds in smaller yards and back gardens behind the houses, and provide counselling for beginners, how they can start gardening on a small plot of land, even a few square meters. A few years ago a film was made of urban gardens with the title Growing Cities[15], which answers quite a few questions why it is worth producing vegetables even on a small parcel of land.

However, the emphasis is not on vegetable production, but the planning of our weekly or monthly diet, quite a few websites and applications can help in this process. They mostly assist us in monitoring, testing how much money we spend or save, while others help in how much weight we can lose, or how we can keep our weight.

These are useful tools in the forming and developing of our conscious thinking, and we will present them later.

Food self-sustainability has many benefits:

1. We stay healthy.
2. We do not pay the profit of merchants from whom we bought healthy or unhealthy food, so more money remains on our bank account. So we do not produce loss, i.e. waste for ourselves, and profit for others, i.e. the merchants.
3. We can get rid of the fat on our body, which is waste causing diseases, as medicine regards obesity as a disease in itself.
4. Self-sufficient people do not or scarcely produce waste, which is beneficial
   for the environment.

Concerning point 4., it is enough to refer to one of the biggest problems of our times, namely free plastic bags available in the majority of supermarkets. As self-sustaining people do not or rarely go shopping to the supermarket, they do not accumulate plastic bags and do not pollute the environment, however strangely it may seem, does a lot for nature and the fauna, mostly sea animals. Plastic bags reach the sea and get as far as Antarctica, and as they degrade in about 500 years, and still pollute the environment when the buyer and their offspring are long dead. Many do not even know that there are two artificial islands in the seas consisting of plastic bags and other plastics, e.g. plastic bottles, one is the Eastern Garbage Pile near Japan, while the other, the Western Garbage Pile is near Hawaii. Both of them are famous for integrating our own waste as well. Hopefully, this global problem is solved by the market entry of the startup company ByFusion, which is able to transform unwanted sea waste into building materials[16], in addition on the site, establishing an environmentally friendly production process.

However, today there are only few conscious people, so, in order to have a more efficient solution for an environmental problem, sometimes we must help. This has happened lately in England[17], where since a new regulation was introduced in 2015 plastic bags were only available for money in supermarket chains, and in a year 85 percent less bags were taken away than before. It seemed it was too expensive, therefore it was not bought, however every product was taken home. This is really thought-provoking and highlights how egoist people are, and how indifferent they are, when there is no profit in it for them.

Self-sufficiency does not only include food production. Many would not think how many everyday objects we could make ourselves, ordinary people. For instance, detergents and wash-up liquids, personal hygiene items, e.g. our deodorant, toothpaste or soap, the latter even from used cooking oil.

Many people, not thinking about a better solution pour used oil in the sink or the toilet, although in many countries used oil can be collected. However, in our devil-may-care world 'there is no time for that', so the waste flows into the drain. The concentrated waste may even develop into a fat mountain underground, as it happened in London a few years ago[18], causing quite a few environmental concerns for the city and taxpayers, as the costs of disposal has to be paid by taxpayer money. Meanwhile, conscious people recycle oil at home, and they can even make scented home-made soap with herbs[19]. In this case we have done nothing else, but recycled waste. Unfortunately, not everybody recycles, so obviously there will be fat mountains in the gutter for a long time.

Of course, critiques can note that when the soap is used, the original cooking oil will flow into the gutter anyway, where is the solution? Of course, they are in part right, and that drains are unsustainable, other solutions would be needed, e.g. residential houses, which operate compost toilets, but this is a different story.

In the appropriate parts of our book we give you tips how you can save your household expenditures by self-sufficiency, and how we can live better and more meaningfully. However, we cannot provide exact calculations, how much one can save a month, but we can show you the proportions, and we reckon for a person becoming self-aware it is enough. And those, who take it up, can invent many things themselves, find tricks on the internet, and applying new ideas, besides resulting in huge savings, can also give us a feeling of success.

Reforming our train of thoughts and applying appropriate behavioral patterns – the significance of resources

If we place light switches low in our flat, our three-year-old child can reach it, and we can teach them to switch off the light when they leave their room. We can save some electricity, but not only this is important. It is also important that the child learns what waste is, what appropriate resource management is already when they are three. Lightning without function is no other but wasted energy, or waste. For the child to be able to reach the switch, we need to be conscious too, so as to form or transform our personal space that the child can have access to energy use. For this, it is necessary to reform our own thinking and behavior, not only to raise the child appropriately, but also to be able to exploit this knowledge in other areas of life as well. For instance, we can collect rainwater and water our high flowerbed, so the rainwater does not become 'waste', but a power giving life and it is for free. Meanwhile, in the majority of households it flows away, as we do not build tools to collect them. Eventually, by saving electricity and using rainwater we do nothing else but manage our resources appropriately, as we have to preserve them for future generations, this is the only way of sustainable development.

However, the majority of consumers are not conscious, their apartments or houses are fully illuminated in the night, which is unintentionally, but well depicted by the wonderful video[20] of NASA, which shows the Earth during the night. On the video it is apparent that North America and Europe are full of light during the night, similarly to other 'developed' areas in the world. Is so much light necessary, or would less be sufficient?

Of course, less would be sufficient, however, we do not live consciously, do not change our habits, so according to our estimate, 40-50 percent of the electricity is wasted, i.e. it is waste. Arizona organization The International Dark-Sky Association does not take 40-50 percent waste (electric power), yet its data are quite convincing[21].

Talking about electricity consumption, we must talk about the standby function, and it makes us understand why America or Europe is fully illuminated during the night. Or we can approach the problem this way: are you also in this 80 billion dollar waste business?

According to the 2013 report by the IEA (International Energy Agency) [22] the annual consumption of office and home appliances also operating in standby mode, mostly consoles, computers and televisions could be decreased significantly, however it does not in spite of targeted awareness-raising campaigns. Why? People do not think appropriately, and do not switch off their appliances when they do not use them anymore. Apparently, the harmful consequence does not concern them that they spend more money on energy than they should. How much does it cost annually? Altogether 80 billion USD. If consumers had a more conscious attitude and manufacturers also used appropriate technologies by which the appliances could switch off themselves, 65 percent of the energy could be saved. If consumers stay negligent, and we do not think their habits will significantly change until 2020, the annual 80 billion USD my increase to 120 billion. According to estimates, 50 billion appliances will connect to the grid by then.

We could cry from pain if we consider that with this pointless devastation we blow away the Earth, as we overshot year by year, we consume our annual resources a lot earlier than December 31st. In a finite system, to believe that infinite consumption can prevail is quite naïve. However, this does not concern the average consumer, it does not even occur to them they should consider this. However, the moment will come, maybe before 2050, when we will have to declare the system is not sustainable anymore. The question is what will happen then.

The significance of appropriate, considerate planning and adaption

Those who wish to give up waste production do not even have to emphasize how important it is to start planning their days or even their lives smartly, and when problems arise, adapt appropriately. For instance those who take up growing vegetables have to decide whether they wish to do it in their back yard, enter an urban gardening community, or a third option join community agriculture. This brings about a series of decisions, which does not bring the expected results in case of wrong planning. The proof of the pudding is in the eating, so when someone wants to move to the countryside once and for all, and produce their own food there partly or completely, before taking the decision, it is worth trying whether they can pursue life in the countryside. If they spend a few weeks on a farm and try sometimes hard physical work, they will see whether they can do it or not.

Of course, people can never take completely appropriate decisions perfect for any need, and also problems may arise which must be solved. For instance, when someone decides to say goodbye in their urban back yard to the lawn and build high beds instead to produce basic, if possible, chemical-free vegetables, they have to struggle with the bugs and fungi, which have the same purpose: eat the harvest. Sometimes this struggle seems to be vain, but the greatness of humans is exactly that. They can overcome the difficulties, and use better methods year by year to trick fungi or bugs.

If others manage to maintain self-sufficiency, we should not give up either, let us think about successful urban gardeners, e.g. the Dervaes family[23]. In the eighties Jules Dervaes bought a house needing renovation in Pasadena, and started to farm in order to be self-sustainable, in his not too big, 4300 ft^2 garden. In the first few years he was able to provide a few vegetables for the family, but today they produce over two and a half tons of food with the family annually. The surplus is frozen for the winter or sold, for about 20 thousand USD. They also have livestock, and produce dairy products, yoghurt, butter from the milk, and they also bake their own bread. They do not only produce food, but try to achieve complete self-sufficiency. They use solar cells, so their electricity bill last year was only 12 dollars. Of course, they achieve these results not only through technology, but by changing their way of life. When they need light, they light with olive oil and own-produced wax candles, as they have bees to fertil-ize their crops. They also have manual mixers, and a solar powered oven, so that they can save energy appropriately. They scarcely watch television and they rather care for each other and form a real, human community. They operate their car, if they use it at all, with cooking oil received from the neighboring restaurants, but they rather walk or cycle. They produce their own beauty and home care products, and cut each other's hair, when necessary, and they buy their clothes in second-hand shops, or exchange them. They use herbs instead of pharmaceuticals, when they are rarely ill. They keep a blog of their lifestyle and experiences, which is of great help for those who are just taking up self-sufficiency.

We could characterize their lifestyle by saying they do not pro-duce waste at all, what they can recycle and reuse, save their resourc-es and by that, they also make quite a lot of money. The key to their success is extremely conscious planning, constant adaption and a radical change of behavior.

We can add that they use only as many objects as they need, and only those which are useful in some way, i.e. none of them is waste.

Almost waste, things without function

We could ask the question, whether everything we do not use qua-si constantly, is waste?

When we look around in the apartment, there are quite a few things collected we had paid for some time ago, yet they scarcely have any function or do not use them at all. This is especially true for the clothes of an average person in a welfare society.

In accordance with the ever-changing fashion, many of our clothes live almost their complete life in the wardrobe in a half-dead state. When we make a list of them with their prices if we still remember, we may face a huge sum, even thousands of dollars, what we spent in vain during the years. Of course, there is no need to exaggerate, and we need to shop when necessary, however we need to consider whether we need so many clothes later, or thinking consciously and planning our lives, we give up regular shopping considered so usual and normal in consumer society.

Canadian journalist Sarah Lazarovic[24] did so; she did not buy any clothes for a year, and then wrote a book about it, with the title 'A Bunch of Pretty Things I Did Not Buy'[25]. The book became a bestseller soon. Not only because it is an interestingly edited book, but because it called the attention to the fact that eventually shopping does not stop the depression of unhappy people, only eases it for some time.

Similarly to Sarah, unnecessary consumption has made many people start thinking, for instance Andrew Hyde, who also tried in practice how many pieces of clothes we need to live happily and well. The number is shocking[26]. Hyde says 15 pieces are sufficient. We can say that Andrew Hyde is an interesting person. One day he decided to sell everything and what remained he put in a backpack and travelled around the world. He wrote a blog on the journey, which he later published as an e-book[27], but he did not become famous because of that, but because he freed himself from the captivity of everyday objects. Hyde says constant shopping will not make us happy, but other things will. When we shop we do nothing else but collect things in our home resembling a warehouse which we will not or only scarcely use. In addition, the given object makes us happy only for a short time, so to gain happiness we shop again and again, and it becomes a vicious circle, and the pile of waste becomes higher and higher.

Based on Hyde's supposition we can start thinking that similarly to clothes, how many of our objects we had bought are unnecessary, and how many we plan to buy in the future and treat them as waste practically. We can consider how much money we have paid for these goods, and we can also add how much we will not pay for the new ones.

In life, there can be interesting occurrences, when we cannot decide whether the given object is already waste or not. Of course, the scorched grass in California from droughts does not fulfil the function expected by the consumer, i.e. to provide the view of a beautiful green lawn; however, it cannot be considered waste, as grass is capable of renewal. Meanwhile, due to the lack of water only little water can be used for watering and unnecessary use of water is also sanctioned, so when owners want nice green lawns around the house, they need to apply other solutions. At least this is what nifty homeowners do, when they paint the grass green around the house[28], thus solving the problem.

It is likely that ventures painting the grass green will flourish in the next decades, as due to the unlimited water consumption earlier, the lack of water is constant in California, well-illustrated by the photos[29] taken of the desertification of the US state in 2015. On the photos it is visible that residential buildings and their yards are still green, however, the areas between the districts have become dust bowls. How could this happen[30]? Well, not only due to watering of the green lawns. It is due to two major factors: agriculture consuming too much water and the unlimited need of the American way of life for consumption.

If we want to have water all the time and have a green environment as well, obviously we need to save water, as we cannot know when, similarly to the US state, the water base underneath us will start to decrease dramatically. The correct selection of our thinking and behavioral patterns should not only concern the present, but the future as well, when the real problem has not even outlined yet.

If we think appropriately, we may even save the Earth, even if we do not have to fear that we will run out of water in the near future. At least this is what two British university students thought, who came forward with the proposition in 2014 that during our morning shower we should pee into the drain[31], and by this we can save flushing the toilet in the morning. The students said their campaign divided the public; some loved the idea, while others hated it. However, their real objective with the campaign was not only to encourage the Brits to save water in this manner, although annually a significant amount of water, 720 million liters could be saved by the public, but to challenge conventional behavior and provoke a debate about the resource which is taken for granted, although it is not. The two students also called the attention that the real saving is not using better and more and more economical objects, it is only a half-victory, but changing our habits and way of thinking.

Obviously the idea of the two students will never be realized, however other ideas can be implemented in practice, however, it can be a good example how another infrastructure, not the shower, can be used, and how one can make a little money by it.

Exploiting unused infrastructure or equipment

Talking about flushing the toilet, we can remain at this topic. Everyone can let their toilet if others are willing to rent it. This business model, which started in the US might sound bizarre, however in places where there are a lot of tourists or visitors and there is no restaurant or mall nearby, it may work well. The idea of the service was born in 2014 in New Orleans, during the Mardi Gras festival organized each year. The number of public toilets was not sufficient for the crowd reaching hundreds of thousands, and they were not clean enough, so Travis Laurendine and Max Gaudin made an app, which helps tackling the problem. The application Airpnp[32] based on Airbnb and Uber fulfilled the hopes in spite of the doubts, although many did not think this may be a successful business model. The doubters probably are reluctant to share their toilets, which is quite understandable, however many did not think so and their way of thinking was unconventional.

Apparently, the digital revolution has helped the development of the economy based on sharing, and this is how Hoffice[33] started, almost at the same time as the toilet sharing app, in 2013, and started spreading in the world. It is also based on a very simple idea. While the person letting the place works at their workplace, or at home, but would share their home with others, let it to others from 8 in the morning until 5 in the afternoon. Who can benefit from this? Those, who would not like to work at home, alone, as in a 'jailhouse', or look for a cheap office for a few employees, and would like to benefit from community life; for them an office in the neighborhood, shared with others and thus having a low rental fee is ideal.

It is not our only concern, whether the Hoffice movement, otherwise labelled environmentally friendly, is successful, but the fact that we should reconsider what the part of our property which is not inhabited or used signifies from the aspect of waste management. Generally, such an area does not produce profit at all, only loss, eventually waste, as if it cannot be solved technically otherwise, such an area has to be heated during the winter and cool during the summer. Thus it is worth considering, if we do not live in a property of which every square meter is more or less exploited, it is worth to change, or initially buy or rent one, which fulfils our needs, yet every square meter is exploited. If we do not do so, we can calculate how much money is lost monthly or even annually.

This may even be a higher sum, to which smaller daily or weekly sums can be added. Many do not even consider these things, although many a little makes a mickle.

Many a little makes a mickle

This is one of the most important principles, yet we often ignore it. However, we should take it into consideration, as in waste management we should not think about 5-10 minute periods, but months, or even years if we wish to save much.

We can illustrate this with an everyday example how we can save money, while not producing waste, as the best waste is waste not even produced.

When we travel, for instance from one city to the other, we often buy mineral water or soda expensive, a lot more expensive than as if we bring it along. At filling stations, movie theaters, beaches or other public places water or soda costs at least twice as much as in smaller shops, or even three times more when we buy these drinks in bigger bottles, in large department stores. When I was not a conscious customer, I used to pay more for water during lunchtime at my workplace five times a week, 1 dollar for half a liter, approximately 260 dollars total in a year. When I started to buy the same water by 10 liters in the store and take the refilled half liter plastic bottle, I saved 50 cents on every half a liter, i.e. I paid half for the same amount of water as in the restaurant before. It is not difficult to calculate that I could save 130 dollars a year by this simple solution, which is quite a big sum. Especially, when we take into consideration that there are many products we buy regularly, e.g. other bottled drinks, snacks, chocolate, ice cream, on which we can also save in this manner, and when we take these into consideration, a really high sum can be saved in a year, or even monthly.

In the meantime, this sum can even be increased when, staying with our example, we produce our lunch ourselves and eat it during lunch break, and do not buy unhealthy snacks, sugary sweets or sodas and similar products during the day. When I started taking lunch I almost fully produced myself to my workplace, in this case, ratatouille with rice, it made me smile that I only paid for the rice I could not produce,

approximately 25 cents, while others paid about 5 dollars for their lunch. With this method, in a year I could have saved 1235 dollars annually and approximately 95 dollars monthly, if I had worked every workday, and eaten food produced by myself. Unfortunately, I did not eat food produced by me every day, and not always rice of course, but in the majority of time, approximately in two thirds of the year I ate the food I produced. However, it is not our goal to calculate everything exactly, but by highlighting the proportions to show why it is worth saving based on the principle 'many a little makes a mickle'.

When we consider in our calculation that we spend in average approximately 2 dollars on the aforementioned unhealthy food and snacks, it is not difficult to calculate that we waste 520 dollars annually, about 43 dollars monthly on these products, also producing a significant amount of waste in the meantime. If we add that we drink sugary sodas or energy drinks, we may also spend approximately 2 dollars a day, and this may also add up to 520 dollars a year, about 43 dollars a month. So if we only calculate with water, unhealthy and other snacks and sugary sodas, we spend 130 + 520 + 520 dollars annually, which amounts to 1270 dollars, which is about 100 dollars a month. Practically, we pay a lot more, as we do not drink only half a liter of water at our workplace, and we also buy sandwiches there, drink coffee, etc.

Why is it interesting, and why have we calculated in such a detail?

When we add these costs, we also face the fact that these costs are more than as if we bought a product in the meantime we consider quite expensive. If we want to buy a shirt for 100 dollars, we do not consider it cheap, and we could buy even a dozen, if we had not wasted our money on the products mentioned above. Cheap products are not considered expensive according to our value system, so we spend our money on them without thinking, yet these are the most expensive goods.

In addition, because of these unhealthy foods sooner or later we may suffer from diseases, i.e. we can say while we go bankrupt, as we spend a lot more than necessary, we even pay for becoming ill.

We can take notes on how much money we spend daily, and in the process a website can also help us, on which we can update what we spent money on. We can promise it will be a shock for many. Websites can also provide applications we can download on our smartphones[34], so our necessary documentation can be always at hand.

However, our calculations do not end here. We also have to take into consideration the amount of waste a person becoming conscious does not produce during a certain period. When I only have to buy one half-liter plastic bottle in the beginning of the year, not five a week, and then refill it regularly, I did not have to throw out 259 plastic bottles in the bin. Of course, I had to buy the 10 liter plastic bottles, so I loaded the environment, or the two garbage piles in the ocean, with that amount of plastic[35], however after a year our circle of friends started to collect water from a spring, so I did not even produce this waste later, as the best waste is waste not produced, and in addition I did not even have to pay for the 10 liter product in the store. Meanwhile, I had to share the costs of the car, when I went to buy water or when it was delivered. The source was found about 10 miles from home. Going there and back took 20 miles, but usually four of us travelled together. The fuel is 1 gallon on the 20 miles, costing about 2.3 dollars, but as four of us travelled together, the costs are shared by four. It is easy to calculate that travel costs and the cost of getting water is a little more than half a dollar per person. [36]

Many a little makes a mickle, and when we save, no waste is produced.

Of course, we can argue that water is not cool in summer, and we cannot always take the bottle with us, as it does not always fit into our handbag. Meanwhile, we can overcome these problems, when there is a will, there is a way. We have not heard about any handbag in which bottles can be cooled, but it is not the purpose, we want to take not only our water, but our daily food, coffee, and who knows what to our workplace. American housewife Melissa Kieling[37] also faced this problem when she was thinking where to put the snacks of her children when they were going to school. As she could not find a suitable solution on the internet, she made a bag, which was able to keep foods cool for 10 hours. The product became a hit, and Melissa became a millionaire. She really needed it, as she launched the cooler bag soon after she divorced her husband, and she only had 13 dollars on her account.

Those who do not calculate with the principle of many a little makes a mickle, and how much money they spend in vain, are not aware how much waste they produce annually. And we produce really much, we are swimming in waste, about which a photographer, Antoine Repessé[38] took spectacular picture, though he did not base his work on one year, but four. The photos are shocking; it is enough to have a look.

It can be considered an investment

There can be household appliances, which might be more expensive than similar products, yet it is worth buying them, as they are cheaper to run, and after a while they can return the money it was spent on them. However, people are likely to buy the cheapest product, which does not prove to be efficient, and during the years we pay more than we should. A German startup company also argued with this, which produced a revolutionary solar cell in 2016. According to the laboratory tests, the product of Insolight[39] produces electricity with double efficiency, and obviously it will not be cheap, the double efficiency will soon return the investment.

Buying the same product by performing a price comparison should not be confused with the example above. After thorough study, we can order the same product from another merchant. It is not worth buying the first product we see if we can suppose it may be cheaper elsewhere, especially when there is a coupon available for the purchase.

From cradle to cradle

In waste management, besides the principle of Everything goes somewhere there is another important principle, the From cradle to cradle principle. Earlier, the From cradle to grave principle was used, incorrectly, when the lifecycle of a product was modelled, including the disposal of the product becoming waste. Accumulating and incinerating waste is a huge cost, cost, by which environmental pollution can be eliminated, or environmental damages mitigated. In order to avoid environmental damage, according to the From cradle to cradle principle the industry should produce products, which, supposing the given cycle, as we have mentioned earlier, return to nature. Such products can be the plantable sneakers[40] for instance, edible plates[41] and cutlery[42], plantable pencils[43] or toothbrushes[44], biodegradable beer
bottles[45], edible glasses[46], and many other interesting objects.

Today we cannot answer the question when we will reach the idealistic state, and when will all our objects biodegradable. We still have to wait for long, at least as long as our society is built on fossil fuel.

Waste not produced is the best waste

For average people it is often difficult to imagine waste not produced, as they consume all day, and in their thinking the waste they produce is not represented, or how much money they could save, as they do not focus on anything else but consuming. If this idea appeared and they acted accordingly, our society would be ideal, and we should not have written this book either.

Originally it was a popular slogan of environmentalists that Waste not produced is the best waste, but today it has infiltrated everyday life, and has gained a peculiar meaning. Its main message for the consumer is that if we do not buy, waste is not even produced. Or when we do not switch on the light unnecessarily, or we turn off the tap while shaving. Or a good example for this is not buying a plastic bottle of mineral water as we have mentioned earlier. Even this plastic bottle would not have been necessary if I had been a conscious customer, and had retrieved the glass bottle from my grandmother's basement, being there unused for a decade, which would have been useful for my purpose. As I have been using this for a long time and I drink spring water I do not produce further waste anymore, unlike others. They could also get a few bottles and use a water cleaner device[47], which filters tap water and drink it all day. If some of them reads this book may change, if not for having less waste in the environment, but to save money.

Of course, the question arises if everybody was conscious and would not consume, would not buy mineral water producing piles of waste every day, what would happen? Would producers go bankrupt? Probably, but this is not the interest of the consumer society, or the states operating these societies, as this society is fueled by constant economic growth. At least, many think so.

Even a living being can be waste not produced?

It is a strange question, of course it could be, but in the consumer society exactly the opposite is true. Easter bunnies or other pets as surprise presents are the best examples. Pets bought expensively as a present may be abandoned, their ignorant and cruel owners may leave them near the road, however, they could take them to animal shelters instead. Refusing a gift might be considered impolite, and the pets suffer from this human behavior. Although animal rights advocates call the attention every year not to buy pets unnecessarily, they cannot reach their goal. Shopping fever, coupled with the desire to be happy seeing our loved ones to be happy, overwrites every rational thought. Similarly to the shame of the person who is given the present not to refuse the gift, as it is simpler to get rid of the helpless pet than to explain the person giving the gift that we are not prepared for keeping a pet. Of course, the biggest responsibility is that of the person giving the gift, as they should try to give a present, which is welcomed by the person receiving the gift. However, it is not a custom to discuss what the gift should be. From the point of view of waste management it should be obvious.

We should consider what proportion of the gifts received for birthdays, Christmas or the good old Valentine's we should not get rid of or keep in the apartment unnecessarily, if the person giving the gift knew that the gift was obsolete.

Recycling

There are many pages dealing with recycling of various objects on the net, their majority is quite creative, however, to recognize for a lifetime how important recycling is, we should have a look on an absolutely creative, perhaps the most creative solution[48] in this field. The picture shows a wagon spanning over a mountain stream in Georgia, serving as a bridge for those passing along the path between Khertvisi and Akhalkalaki. Obviously, it could not have been easy, let alone figure out it would be much simpler to cross through a piece of worthless waste instead of building a costly bridge.

NOTES:

1. *https://www.youtube.com/watch?v=3QZp6smeSQA - https://www.laca.org.au/ index.php/biodiversity/ecosystem-services/638-cardboard-to-caviar-biomicry*

2. *http://www.georgianjournal.ge/discover-georgia/30231-in-soviet-georgia-the-story-behind-the-cult-yogurt-ad.html*

3. *https://www.youtube.com/watch?v=oFBAwzTl-gY*

4. *http://www.greenhome.com/business/green-food-service-supplies/hot-cup-lid.html*

5. *https://www.theguardian.com/environment/2016/mar/15/ coffee-cup-britons-3-billion-so-few-recylced*

6. *https://www.youtube.com/watch?v=uRGiGbX9llo*

7. *http://www.news.com.au/finance/starbucks-takes-on-nespresso-in-coffee-war/ news-story/aa487841ed27844bfb6a74e02400d993*

8. *http://fortune.com/2016/06/10/starbucks-card-balance/*

9. *https://www.terracycle.com/en-US*

10. *http://www.centennialbulb.org/index.htm*

11. *https://en.wikipedia.org/wiki/Planned_obsolescence*

12. *http://documentarylovers.com/film/the-lightbulb-conspiracy/*

13. *https://www.youtube.com/watch?v=tAKC5KEFwh4*

14. http://victorygardeninitiative.org//

15. http://www.growingcitiesmovie.com/the-film/

16. https://www.youtube.com/watch?v=Dtp-k8YsIOM

17. http://www.bbc.com/news/science-environment-36917174

18. https://www.youtube.com/watch?v=SOwi868XtL8

19. https://beauty.onehowto.com/article/how-to-make-soap-with-used-oil-1505.html

20. https://www.youtube.com/watch?v=EPyl1LgNtoQ

21. http://cescos.fau.edu/observatory/lightpol-econ.html

22. http://www.iea.org/publications/freepublications/publication/MoreData_LessEnergy.pdf

23. http://urbanhomestead.org/

24. http://longliveirony.com/

25. http://www.penguin.com/book/a-bunch-of-pretty-things-i-did-not-buy-by-sarahlazarovic/9780143124719 - http://www.huffingtonpost.com/2014/10/27/sarah-lazarovic-book-interview_n_6017260.html

26. http://andrewhy.de/the-15-things-i-own/

27. http://thisbookisabouttravel.com/

28. https://www.youtube.com/watch?v=Wgj8QOCQOoE

29. http://www.ara.cat/fotografies/Piscines-al-desert_5_1339716017.html

30. http://www.wnd.com/2015/09/experts-california-drought-fire-crisis-man-made/

31. http://www.bbc.com/news/uk-england-norfolk-29552557?_ga=1.113905615.916
690107.1407856939

32. https://thenextweb.com/apps/2014/03/04/airpnp-its-like-airbnb-but-for-toilets/#.
tnw_YtuGfeaA

33. http://hoffice.nu/en/what-is-hoffice/

34. https://play.google.com/store/apps/details?id=mic.app.gastosdiarios&hl=en

https://play.google.com/store/apps/details?id=com.mhriley.spendingtracker&hl=en

https://play.google.com/store/apps/details?id=com.handyapps.expenseiq.

35. http://www.huffingtonpost.com/norm-schriever/post_5218_b_3613577.html

36. As the spring was situated about 10 miles away from our home, we did not
have to travel a long distance to deliver the required amount of water home. All this
amounted to only a few dollars, but even that was divided, depending on how many
people had to transport water at a time.

37. http://www.cnbc.com/2014/08/26/from-broke-mom-to-multimillion-dollar-suc-
cess.html

38. https://www.worldphoto.org/sony-world-photography-awards/
winners-galleries/2016/professional/shortlisted/campaign/antoine

39. http://phys.org/news/2016-09-startup-residential-solar-panels-efficient.html

40. http://www.core77.com/posts/18541/
oat-shoes-biodegradable-sneakers-thatsprout-18541

41. http://www.psfk.com/2015/09/edible-plates-do-eat-sustainable-tableware.html

42. https://www.kickstarter.com/projects/1240116767/
edible-cutlery-the-future-of-eco-friendly-utensils

43. http://sproutworld.com/us/

44. https://www.youtube.com/watch?v=DbY7Nn8-S-8

45. http://qz.com/331879/carlsberg-may-soon-be-serving-beer-in-cardboard-bottles/

46. http://loliware.squarespace.com/e

47. http://www.walmart.ca/en/ip/brita-grand-pitcher-white/926943

48. http://www.messynessychic.com/2013/09/04/the-treachurous-train-bridge/

Chapter 2 - Wasteful consumption is the core of consumer society

'I rationalize shop. I buy a dress because I need change
for gum.'
/Rita Rudner, American comedian/

Everything is decided in the mind, they say. It is especially true when we would like to save by decreasing our costs and expenditures, and live well from less. To reach this goal, first we have to tidy up our thoughts, we need to be able to control the stubborn consumer living inside of us. The stubborn consumer urges us to shop, own, consume, shop again, waste again until we can, without limits. However, if we become conscious, and we can stop these urges, we can become conscious customers, who can live a rich and wealthy life.

This lifestyle is not only characterized by a nice sum on our bank account, but by something else as well: a conscious person will not or only scarcely produce waste.

HISTORICAL OVERVIEW

About 100-150 years ago, in the so-called developed world the value system was totally different. We can say people only consumed what they need at the moment, therefore consumption was in balance with needs. Farmers were usually self-sufficient, and with a little exaggeration we can say that a farmer only went to the shop to buy petroleum and salt, and did not produce, or scarcely produced any waste. This balance was not disturbed by cities either, there was no need for overconsumption, which later radically transformed agricultural production and also waste production.

However, when oil and natural gas appeared as energy sources, everything changed, and society became dependent on fossil fuel, and in parallel the consumer, who wants more and better all the time appeared. Oil, if we look back on the past 100 years, has become an extremely successful energy source, and did not only conquer transportation in a short time, but also started to dominate the industry and agriculture, then with the dumping of plastic made of oil it has conquered the world, by now causing gigantic environmental pollution on the planet. A hallmark of this process is plastic waste pouring everywhere, new waste piles emerging near cities every day and the huge islands of waste floating on the seas.

Due to oil, which was considered cheap for decades, after the world economic crisis in 1939 and WWII the economy started to grow again, or in other words, started to follow a coerced growth track; the consumer society appeared, in which the consumer, to avoid another crisis, felt safe when there was peace, and the economy grew year by year. It is by no accident that the government program of any country has been about nothing else but economic growth. Of course, America led this process, which is followed, no matter what nonsense it is, by developing countries like China or India as well.

An American scientist, Richard Heede made a list of corporations[1] involved in oil, natural gas and coal exploitation in 2013, which pollute the planet the most. The study surprised even Heede himself. As he summarized, the number of the real polluters is not really high, only 90 corporations, however, these are the companies which contribute to global warming and climate change significantly by their carbon emissions.

Yet we should not forget about the fact why companies do this. Of course, they do this for the profit, but not only for that. The consumer wants to consume, and it has to be fulfilled, so not only corporations are to be held responsible for unwanted tendencies, especially environmental pollution and climate change, but the consumers behind them as well. The consumer, whether they want it or not, is part of the system, and talking about oil, they are the ones who, due to their habits do not only fill the bin every day with garbage, but by their daily car use, they also fill the sky with waste. Normally, carbon dioxide, as human waste should have nothing to do in the atmosphere. However, consumers contribute to gas emissions by 20 percent annually only as a result of their transportation, which is a shocking proportion itself. Interestingly, carbon dioxide cannot be seen in the air, so many do not think it even exist, similarly to the problem caused by it. However, when carbon emission is depicted on an image[2], it can be seen in the given picture that the Empire State Building is almost fully covered by waste colored in blue, and we are shocked how much garbage we throw at the sky every day.

By the last third of the 20th century, the American way of life became a model to follow all over the world, which meant a huge house, several cars, a good workplace and a thick account in a bank. When any American family reached that, they could consider themselves happy and successful. At least this was the appearance, and this prevails in spite of the fact that in 2008 a significant economic and financial crisis shocked the world, especially the US, and questioned the idea whether everybody is safe who is part of the consumer society.

In the society transforming after WWII, money accumulated as a result of economic growth had to be spent, and we can say that in capitalism, which is global today, everything is for sale. There is nothing which cannot be bought.

This was made easy by the fact that people, when they can afford it, start wasting. Wasting can be matched to the profit hunger of giant corporations entering the market in the past 100 years, so sales and consumption started to amplify each other, almost imperceptibly. Trade provides what the consumer needs, and consumers buy not only what trade offers, but what they do not need at all. In other words, they waste.

WASTING IS A PROGRAM ENCODED IN OUR GENES?

If we believe waste only characterizes our times, we are wrong. This behavior characterized us already in the Stone Age. At least, this is proven by the Stage Three Project[3] study carried out in 2012, which explored the relationship between homo sapiens, the new man and the environment. According to the study, at the habitats of the homo sapiens, a lot more mammoth bones were found than at the habitats of the Neanderthal, which, according to scientists, is attributed to more efficient hunting due to new technical equipment and planning. Homo sapiens realized after a while that mammoths defend themselves successfully on open fields, but if they can herd the animals into a ravine, they can hunt them down more easily by throwing stones and spears. Although the hunting, taking into consideration the significant volume of meat of the animal would have been successful in case one animal was hunted down, excavations prove that the horde killed several animals at the same time, in spite of the fact that they could not eat so much meat.

So why was this necessary?

Ronald Wright, in his book The Short Story of Development[4] and in the film adaptation of the book also dealt with mammoth hunting as a negative example, drawing more complex conclusions, claiming human civilizations cannot survive abundant periods following technical advancement. By hunting down and killing the mammoth, human civilizations started to develop and then declined, and people had to find new solutions for survival, otherwise they would have starved to death. The process started again. The author says that meanwhile newer and newer technologies were developed, our one-time primate brain could not develop as it should have in the past few millennia, the software did not update, so man, although they created successful civilizations from time to time, they failed one after the other, as sooner or later, as a pest, they devoured the environment. Although they started again and again, the later experiments also failed.

Based on the example it is clear that the need for waste is encoded in our genes, as we are still predators who consider food as a basic necessity, in our times the immediate purchase of consumer goods, and the immediate fulfilment of the need. In this process, reason is missing, there is only a desire for unlimited destruction, which overwrites sensible thinking. Basically we are still similar to the Stone Age man, although we do not hunt down mammoths, but shop in supermarkets and malls, and lately through the internet.

Of course, reading these lines many might be outraged how we can compare the thinking of the man of today and that of the Stone Age. However, it is not difficult, we only need to refer to some animals which can be hunted, to feel what sort of exploitation we pursue today. It is common knowledge today, that 80 percent of sea fish is overfished. Mostly predator fish with delicious meat like sturgeon, tuna and sharks are the most endangered species, and maybe the hunt of the latter is the most outrageous. These animals are hunted only for their fins, so after cutting the fin off, the still living animals are thrown back into the sea like waste. Merchants do not know any limits, they want more and more. To illustrate the need for an animal, which has almost extinct, the blue-fin tuna, we must see that in the beginning of 2015 at the Tokyo fish market 37,500 USD was paid for a 180 kilogram specimen[5]. Of course the consumer, who buys a tin of fish in the supermarket, cannot feel the vastness of this destruction.

Not only fish are endangered, any animal can fall victim and become extinct when the demand increases for them. A good example for this senseless killing is the poaching of rhinoceroses. In spite of all the efforts, when even armed guards are employed to protect these animals, in South Africa the killing of these animals increased further in 2014, when 1215 animals were killed according to the BBC[6]. While in China and India records sums are paid for the rhino horns, these unfortunate animals have little chance to survive, greed wins over rationality.

GREED AND GLUTTONY

Greed and gluttony are negative human traits, and make people easy to manipulate. Merchants, multinational corporations and shopping chains which did not exist 100 years ago, however by now conquering the world know that well, and day by day place new 'baits' in our habitat hunting for new consumers in the form of advertisements, promotions, and computer data in the digital world. It is very difficult to stay neutral and abstain from shopping. However, a conscious customer can 'switch off', and if they cannot be manipulated, will not spend money obsoletely.

They only buy the most necessary items, do not waste unnecessarily. To stop waste it is not necessary to go off-grid and live in a forest, like the Hejlskov[7] family did a few years ago, we have other ways to protect ourselves against the 'attacks' of the globalized world.

Before proceeding, we will explain through an interesting example how easily we can be manipulated by the information applied in advertising day by day that something is for free, i.e. we do not have to pay for it. At a conference about sustainable development, during the break in the lavatories I had to tell two colleagues, trained, conscious environmentalists that it is enough to use two paper towels after washing their hand, not five. First they were shocked, then they felt ashamed when they understood what I was talking about. When I did not even use a paper towel but dried my hands in an old canvas tissue which used to belong to my grandfather, they slapped their forehead why the thought had not occurred to them earlier. I do not buy, I scarcely buy paper tissue, paper towels for the kitchen, and do not buy paper-based devices, as, however incredible it may seem, we can live without them. These things did not exist 50-100 years ago, and human society could survive.

It may still be normative today, so if we did not use tissue papers and other similar, we would not have to destroy the environment by cutting down billions of hectares of forests[8] or would not have to process billions of tons of waste paper[9] daily either. I note for the sake of completeness that everybody paid for the use of the toilet and the paper at the conference, as it was included in the registration fee.

However, I have to tell that I myself do not do it, my partner, who is an everyday consumer, buys paper tissue and paper towels regularly, in spite of our permanent dispute over the matter. She is reluctant to wash the canvas handkerchief we blow our nose in, as she considers it 'disgusting', so we have to collect all the paper waste and incinerate it in the furnace in winter. However, it is only a pseudo-solution, as woods will still be cut down.

Fortunately, others change their habits more easily than my partner, like the software development company from the Netherlands, which wanted to make their office paper-free in 2014. In order to achieve the goal, Decos[10] did not even allow the use of toilet paper, as there is a super modern toilet in the office, which also cleans and dries the person's bottom using the facility. We have no information on how the company staff received the decision, or how much toilet paper cost was saved by the Dutch company in a year. However, we know that these toilets were developed by the Japanese in 1999, where the concept of cleanliness or bathing is completely different than here.

Unlike Decos, company managers are still hardly environmentally conscious, they work on nothing more but making profit constantly. To achieve this, they only have to exploit the greed of consumers, of which we can see quite a few examples. Of these, as several books and films have dealt with the issue, we will highlight the manipulation of supermarkets.

THE SUPERMARKET IS THE SHRINE OF CUSTOMERS

When we go to a supermarket, we only want to buy a few things, and things we generally need. However, merchants do their best to make us buy not only the necessary things, as their aim is to rip us off. Business Insider in its article[11] mentions 15 tiny tricks of manipulation, including, among others, the specific structure of the sales area, the appropriate placement of advertisements and discounts, as well as the slow and calming music, which makes us stay longer and shop.

However, the tricks are not over. It also matters what kind of goods we buy in supermarkets. 100 years ago foods, like milk and dairy, raw meat and sausages or frankfurters were produced by farmers, not corporations. If we encounter the original recipe for frankfurters on Facebook and the ingredients to make this popular food, we will be surprised, as it is nothing similar to the thing we buy in the supermarkets, full of preservatives, flavor enhancers, and all kinds of artificial ingredients, which has nothing to do in the human body, as the majority of these materials is nothing more than waste, and some of them, according to some studies, is straightly harmful for our health. Our surprise is even bigger when we make frankfurter based on the original recipe, as it turns out the taste of frankfurters is completely different from the one available in shops.

Of course, customers want to buy products produced and processed at a farm, supermarkets claim, so it has to be displayed and packaged as if it was from farms, not animal factories. Director Robert Kenner starts his now world-famous film, Food Inc. [12] with this thought, which, besides the presentation of the domination of the food industry by corporations also shows how easily customers can be manipulated. Similarly, Taste the Waste[13] is also a fantastic film, which, besides depicting what food production has become in our global world, also provides factual data on how much food we throw out as waste within a period of time. The data are shocking.

What can we do against food waste? As we have said earlier, by changing our habits and behavior we can do a lot to achieve our goal, and a good example is a French campaign launched two years ago.

In France, a chain store called Intermarché, which does not fit in the pattern started a campaign in 2014, and claims no less in its video for the campaign[14] that ugly vegetables can also be eaten. This was necessary because supermarkets and corporations delivering vegetables and fruits, saying consumers are only willing to buy perfect products, started to sell the same type of vegetables and fruits everywhere, even their size and shape was identical. So tomatoes and apples and even cucumbers are identical on the counters, and the cucumber could not even be more curved than a certain standard. If a specimen did not meet the standard in size or shape, it was thrown into the garbage, forming mountains of waste. The campaign of Intermarché, highlighting this improper practice became very successful, not only because they started to sell these ugly vegetables and fruits 30 percent cheaper, and the sales in supermarkets joining the chain increased by 30 percent, but also because the French understood that wasting food must be stopped.

Similar campaigns were launched in other European countries and the US as well. In 2015 in the US, where three million tons of vegetables and fruits are thrown away due to their size or shape annually, a startup company[15] decided to collect families subscribing to a dedicated list, and collects the ugly vegetables and fruits from farmers which are not received by supermarkets, and delivers them to the families

30-50 percent cheaper. Anybody can join the crowd-funded website Imperfect[16] according to the conditions set. On their first anniversary, the founders wrote in their blogs they saved 700,000 pounds of fruits and vegetables, and the company is growing. Growing?

Initially, they worked with 150 families, now they have 7,500 business partners.

Obviously also due to the campaign of Intermarché, in France a bill[17] was passed in 2015, which forbids wasting food for merchants. In practice, it means expired products cannot be thrown in the garbage, but charity with food has become compulsory, and what has become inconsumable for people, has to be given to animals, or put on the compost. Of course, the proposition was sharply criticized by merchants, as waste management meant extra cost and care, however the government did not mind the protest and passed the bill. It is a question whether the bill will fulfil the hopes, as the bill only sanctions the wasting of supermarkets and not consumers. According to official statistics, the French threw out 20-30 kilograms of still consumable food into the garbage annually before 2015, causing 12-20 billion EUR of damage each year[18]. However, the French did not only ban the wasting of food by supermarkets, another bill was passed in 2016 to curb unlimited wasting, but we will expand on this in the chapter on Household.

BLACK FRIDAY AND DAY OF SINGLES

Black Friday is bringing more and more money in the US and other countries worldwide, which is the traditional kick-off event of the Christmas season. Although shopping coupled with a discount has a century-long history, the name started to spread in 2009. However, this event has not only become renowned because several products were cheaper on this day, but because atrocities during shopping became wide-spread. In addition, in 2008 three deaths occurred on one day, in New York a security guard was crushed to death by customers pouring in a shop before opening in New York[19], while in Los Angeles two people died in a shooting because they had a row during shopping[20]. In China, Black Friday is also popular, only under another name. The Day of Singles, on November 11 was established so that singles without a partner can tell each other why they live alone. However, today this is a feast of the expanding consumer society, mostly due to online orders. While in the US 1.5 billion USD[21] was spent on Amazon and E-Bay in 2015, this number was 9.3 billion on Alibaba[22]. These data illustrate in our globalized world what consumers are able to, and their greed and gluttony can be exploited well by department store chains and online merchants.

Not only gluttony and greed can be exploited, the emotion of happiness is at least as dangerous, which is well-known by merchants and multinational corporations, as well as professionals in the advertising industry. However, this happiness is not the happiness to which many of us associate, what people desire, but something completely else. During shopping people have a nice feeling when they buy themselves this and that. This would not be a problem, but purchasing unnecessary things is a problem, because in that case we do not shop because it is necessary, but because it makes us feel well.

HAPPINESS AND CONSUMPTION

A survey carried out Michigan University in 2014[23] proved that there is a direct relationship between shopping and happiness. The research group claimed no more than unhappy people can be sent to retail therapy instead of prescribing drugs for their depression. If we consider how many unhappy, including depressed people are being treated only in the US today[24], it is not difficult to draw the conclusion what would happen if shopping would be made general as a therapy. The apartments and houses of patients would become huge closets, while their bank accounts would be empty.

ADVERTISEMENTS

Although marketing managers are not psychology graduates, they are really experts in manipulating people. With a little exaggeration, it could be said that they can persuade the majority of people in seconds to form an opinion on the given product they would like them to. And from this point, purchasing is only one step, undoubtedly. What are their methods? I would only list a few from the many, what we need to pay attention to when we are tempted before or during shopping.

Advertisements, which display cute animals or toddlers, naked or barely dressed women, or muscled men, are already suspicious. Their messages are perfectly suitable to manipulate our emotions, so when we see how cute this puppy is in the advertisement, we can easily lose our good reason, and we can hardly concentrate on whether we need the advertised pet food for out pet, we will find it attractive because of its cuteness. However, we can also feel the same, when we see a perfect model in an advertisement, which advertises a perfume, or implies we should buy it, as in a consumer society everybody wants to be perfect. It does not matter whether the given scent suits us, our mind only considers whether we will look as perfectly as the model in the advertisement when we choose the given product. And when we have bought the perfume then realize it does not suit us, we put it in the closet, where it evaporates and becomes nothing more than waste. In this case, nothing else happens, but we wasted money on something we never used.

Advertisements are always present in our lives, especially when we live in the city. On the road, on television, on the radio, and last but not least on the internet as well. We can never get rid of them, as we are always fewer than the intended recipients of the merchants' messages. Al Ries and JackTrout wrote in their book Positioning: Battle for Your Mind[25] that in our accelerated world, consumers' mind is unable to digest as much information as the experts would like them to, so they need to reposition the given products with new and other ideas all the time. For the repositioning of a product often simple, yet effective ideas are sufficient. Probably this was what marketing managers thought who connected the consumption of an otherwise ordinary peanut butter, Jif[26] to elitism. They did nothing more but chose the slogan 'Choosy moms choose Jif'. With this, they provided mothers an experience of belonging to the elite, as what parent would not give the best to their child and thus stand out compared to others. However, why we should choose this peanut butter and not that of the competition, i.e. what the truth is, is not important.

People try to get rid of the majority of advertisements, therefore it is very difficult to call their attention, especially when it is challenging to make an advertising spot about the given product. However, when the advertisement is coupled with a little sense of humor, the product can be embedded in people's minds, and more can be sold of the product. Sometimes even governments, ministries and other bodies try to sell their message with humor, as it can be said in an advertisement with zombies[27].

ARE WOMEN MORE AFFECTED BY ADVERTISEMENTS?

According to traditional belief, women and men have almost totally different shopping habits, e.g. women like shopping better, while men think it is a nuisance, and are reluctant to do it. However, with the spreading of online shopping and gadgets, this concept seems to change, at least a recent survey showed this. The 'Myth of the Mansumer' [28] survey showed with the spreading of the internet, certain customer habits, which could be distributed according to gender, are starting to approach each other, and slowly merge. For instance, both genders are willing to buy films, books and gadgets on the net, as they think online shopping is better, quicker, and last but not least more convenient. However, neither men nor women like when delivery time is too long, or to retrieve information, ordering or payment on the website are too complicated. So far neither men, nor women say goodbye to traditional shops, as women still insist on trying on clothes when shopping, however both genders believe traditional department stores have to improve their services if they want to catch up with the competition, especially, when in the traditional shops shop assistants are untrained, have no technical gadgets, or there is a long queue.

For some time many do not give up their habit and will still shop in traditional shops. However, in an interview to Die Welt in 2015 Mitch Barns[29], the CEO of the biggest market research company of the world, Nielsen talked about dramatic changes. He says today e-traders, e.g. Amazon or Alibaba are not driven by convenience only, when they establish their services on the internet, but they aim to collect as much valuable information about consumers with the help of their unique marketing and advertising strategy, as this new 'industry' makes money from nothing else, but selling customer data. If we have shopped on the given site, or only looked around, the program evaluates it and then the company sells the data to others. These data buyers then can bomb consumers with targeted advertisements and promotion, so the buyer can be fed information in accordance with their interests what and where to buy[30]. Nothing else is necessary, but a smartphone or a tablet, and the internet. It is obvious that due to these technical advancements everyday consumers can be manipulated easily and will buy what they have not wanted, and it is also evident that traditional shops can hardly compete with this. The renowned fashion company American Apparel escaped into bankruptcy partly due to this[31], as the management of the company hardly paid any attention to online sales, and operated several retail units, which were loss-making.

Although the 'Myth of the Mansumer' and Mitch Barns made very fascinating observations, it is undoubted that fitness, health or the beauty industry, similarly to earlier practices, still targets women instead of men with their marketing. Why? The answer is simple. Women are the clients, of whom 90 percent is dissatisfied with their looks, and 40 percent with their weight[32].

Today catwalks are still dominated by super-skinny models, Meaghen Ramsey[33] explains in her presentation, illustrating what pressure fashion can have on women consumer. Every woman has to identify with the trend already when they are teenagers, because if they do not do it, for example they do not diet in their teens, they think they will not fit in their community, they will not be renowned and successful, in other words happy. It is difficult to make a career this way, to find a good job, i.e. be successful in life. The willingness to be similar to stars by teens is best illustrated by the story of a young woman from Britain. Charlotte O'Neill[34] manically wanted to resemble a star, Cheryl Colre, and lost so much weight during her diet that she dropped from 54 kilos to 36, and she could be cured only with a lifestyle change and therapy.

What would happen to the industries above, if one day women realized that they do not have to 'improve' their bodies. They would probably go bankrupt, but this cannot happen obviously, as the thinking and behavior of women in this respect will not or hardly change, positively. However, there are corporations such as Dove[35], which recognized what a problem it is for women that they do not feel themselves beautiful, and started a campaign to prove the contrary. Women presented in their film[36], when they face how positively other people describe them are really moved, and talk among tears they would not have thought others see them beautiful.

In our context, we would like to have an answer to only one question: how much money women spend unnecessarily, and how much waste is produced because 90 percent of them do not feel themselves beautiful and perfect, and 40 percent is dissatisfied with their weight?

Data show women spend 15000 USD on beauty products only until the end of their lives in the US in average[37]. How much money can be spent on clothes and various diets then?

The perfect product however, is not only destined for women, but other customers, e.g. families as well. In an earlier spot, Zewa[38] applied the old recipe for happiness, when they published a 21-second spot on their toilet paper, including the complete list of accessories. Happy and beautiful mother, a son and two daughters, cute kitten, modern and perfect apartment, nothing else is needed for a happy life. Tenderness in every touch, the spot says, and it is not difficult to draw the consequence what the advertisement implies. If we want to be happy, similarly to the family in the video, we should buy exclusively this Zewa product.

However, Zewa has recently added another product to their portfolio, and published an advertising spot[39] which shows an environmentally friendly solution, namely that the core of the toilet roll can be flushed down in the toilet, it melts in seconds. The point is not only this easy solution, but also the fact that the waste does not burden the environment, as it is biodegradable, and dissolves in the canal, unlike the paper core in the garbage. The extent of the problem caused by the core of the toilet paper is shown by the fact that recently a company started to sell toilet paper without core, as waste not produced is the best waste.

According to Kimberley-Clark[40], the world could get rid of 17 billion cores a year
if everybody bought their product. This solution would bring about a double benefit. On one hand, the core would not be produced, so no energy and money would be needed for manufacturing, and as there would not be waste, no management would be needed. In the meantime, it is obvious that the user experience would remain. However, do we remember the solution of the Dutch software developer Decos? They do not use paper in their office at all, which so far seems to be the best solution, if we estimate based on 17 billion rolls how much toilet paper is used by welfare societies globally. Although this specific toilet, which is able to clean the user's bottom is obviously more expensive than the traditional toilet, however it returns the investment after a while, and in the long run it is beneficial for the environment. In this case it is worth considering the cost of operation compared to the price, taking the mere fact into consideration how many times we use the toilet a day.

Although it is apparent which company chose what environmentally-friendly solution during the recent years, it is obvious that there are old and new developments, which offer a better solution to the problem of human feces through recycling. However, this is another story we will write about in the chapter about Household.

THE DIGITAL REVOLUTION

The needs of the consumer society with the appearance of the internet, social media and video sharing sites could be fulfilled more easily than through traditional sales, information has been able to reach a bigger audience in the form of data. By this, many started to say the age of traditional advertising is over, and although in the past 20 years the profession went through major changes, its goal is still targeting consumers with promotion, and it has not changed and will not change either. They still encourage consumption, but with better and more efficient means, e.g. by better or newer smartphones and software on them.

It means not only market trends will significantly change within a few years, but corporations as well. In the middle of 2014, Asus CEO Jonney Shih[41] said there was such a need for immediate information that PC manufacturers could simply become smartphone manufacturers within a few years. The management of Alibaba[42], which became very successful within a short time did not think differently, when they announced in the beginning of 2015 that they would invest 590 million USD in the Chinese startup which will produce an own mobile device for the company, and through its operation system Alibaba will be able to reach its users better and more efficiently.

WHY HAS THE WORLD CHANGED SO MUCH IN SUCH A SHORT TIME? WHY IS THIS URGE?

Data are obvious. By 2017, in the developing world of IoT, 90 percent of the goods will connect to the internet, according to Samsung[43], thus it will be rather worth buying them online. This also means serving customers cannot only be realized through marketing or sales techniques, but via innovative, constantly changing and developing technologies. Mainly, when shopping on the internet is an excellent opportunity for certain webstores[44] to get to know, spy on our shopping habits so that after collecting the data they could bomb us with better, more targeted advertisements, also endangering our privacy. However, development does not stop here, in 2015 a senior manager of Huawei, Wang Yanmin[45] already predicted what smartphones will look like in 2020, or superphones, as the new mobile which is being designed is called that. This smart device will be able to connect the real world with the virtual one, and function as a sort of living organism. It will practically understand people, get to know their habits and behavior. Based on these, it will be able to do mapping in the IoT world, and will send specific data to users, but of course only those which affect the user and what can be needed by them. For instance, when the user gives the voice command to the superphone 'save money', the device will understand immediately and give advice. Of course, this will be possible with the integration of Big data and artificial intelligence.

However, experts say the development of technologies used in traditional retail sales can be big business for companies specialized in these technologies, not only the development of the superphone. In the beginning of 2015 for instance one of the most innovative developments was when mobile wallets, which can be used in traditional retail outlets, were born and started to spread all over the world.

According to consulting company Deloitte[46], while in 2014 less than half percent of customers used the mobile wallet once a month in a retail outlet for payment, this can increase ten times the subsequent year. The need for mobile payment is shown by the fact that in 2016 several US banks started to develop and launch such services. The need for mobile payment is shown by the fact that in 2016 several US banks[47] started to develop and launch such services. But it is not only possible to pay the bills using a smart phone, other smart devices are already able to do this, such as smart fridges developed by MasterCard and Samsung[48], being able not only to order, but to pay for goods. However, the technology does not stop here, as according to Brian Morris, head of Central and Eastern Europe, responsible for innovation in MasterCard payment, within a few years many household devices can connect to the internet and even pay for the ordered devices. However, the still quite expensive fridge is not only interesting because of the payment plan. Since it follows when the respective product will run out, it may encourage us to save, as you can put together your diet based on the order and thinking retrospectively, and this process may later be enhanced by IoT, gaining ground in a few years. So, if you give a diet planning voice control to your smart device, robots will compile it in seconds, adding a shopping list to it, and they can order the goods, pay for them, completing all this at the lowest price.

In the meantime, digitalization will not only affect the development of technology, but will radically transform economy and society as well. Similarly as it happened during the times of the first industrial revolution. As it was also a complex social and economic change, and this transition based on robotics, automation and artificial intelligence is also called revolution, the fourth in a row.

The process is still unrecognizable for many, although it seems to be clear that similarly to the old times, skills are disappearing and new skills are emerging about which we have no notion today. As the CEO of Aon Hewitt said recently[49], from ten children in kindergarten today seven will work in a job which does not exist today. In this age, knowledge becomes outdated a lot sooner, university students[50] who finish their studies in five years will probably not be able to do anything with the knowledge they acquired in the first two years, as new information will be generated, so people will have to learn as long as they live. To this change, which will take place within the next 10-15 years[51], companies also have to adapt, as today the large majority of companies still work in traditional structure and according to traditional values. Their employees go to work every day, work for eight hours a day, then go home when they are finished. This method will be outdated in the world of digitalization, many employees will work from home, no workplaces will be needed. Not only because it will not be necessary to actually go to work, as we can work from home, but also because some jobs can be replaced by robots. For instance, students at the Georgia Technical University did not realize for months that an assistant teacher helping them in their problems was actually an artificial intelligence. The robot based on the software IBM Watson and used as a pilot, with the name Jill Watson[52] answered the questions of students in emails and on forums, quite successfully. It was revealed only after five months, when the students realized the robot answered their questions too quickly, and in addition everybody at the same time. From the funny example it is quite clear which are the jobs which become obsolete in the near future. Such jobs are office and administrative jobs as well as jobs in consulting, however analysts say health care, the energy and the financial sectors may also be affected.

Corporations will have to modernize, as in the world of IoT those companies which have started integration in the new system already work more efficiently and cost-effectively. Only one example of many: one of the most renowned companies in the world, Stanley Black&Decker[53], after applying Cisco Systems products could increase productivity by 92 percent. This data speaks for itself, so probably robots will work in an increasing number of jobs already within the next few years, as this is a lot more cost-effective than employing people in these jobs. In addition, machines are more precise, there are fewer problems than with employees. Of course, there might be disputes whether machines cannot make mistakes, as a semi-automatic car of Tesla is responsible for a fatal accident[54], which occurred in 2016, but is only one drop in the ocean, because news are about 10 million[55] fully or partly self-driving cars on the roads by 2020, depending whether in the given country there are any legal problems related to vehicles without human control. In spite of the expected legal obstacles and approval procedures, the market of pilotless cars has already started to grow rapidly, as according to its announcement in 2016, by 2021 Ford would like to have a dominant role on the market[56] by manufacturing cars without gas or brake pedal, or steering wheel. These all point in the direction that in the next decade, besides private car use taxi riding will also become driverless, which will not be welcomed by dismissed employees, similarly to those, who did not welcome the market entry by Uber who blocked several roads and motorways nationwide in France in 2015, fearing they would lose their jobs and welfare[57]. Although French taxi drivers obviously did not protest against the market entry of self-driving cars, it is evident they can do practically nothing against them, as their jobs will soon be obsolete.

Of course, not only taxi drivers or office clerks become unemployed, regarding the global trend the Economic Forum[58] calculates with the elimination of five million jobs by 2020, and the birth of 2.1 new ones.

What will happen to people who have to leave their jobs?

Some of them will probably be retrained, as in the new world more and more IT people will be needed, however, there will be others who still do not know what will be the jobs they will fulfil. However, who can expect that their jobs will be eliminated, they can do one thing. Besides finding an appropriate job they can do even at home, they can get to know old and new self-sustaining technologies. They can give up their 'wasteful' life, so that they are not surprised by the change, as it happened in 2008 when the global financial crisis hit the US and the rest of the world, depriving many not only of their jobs, but their homes as well. As the world is in transition, it is worth having two strings to your bow, this is the most sensible solution.

How we can start it, we will write about in the next chapter in more detail, here it is enough to refer to a few data how employment changes all over the world. 25 percent of the employees[59], i.e. every fourth person already works from home in the US, Forbes Magazine[60] published the list of the 100 flagship companies in the US in 2016. In the meantime, the number of companies employing distant workers increased by 36 percent in the past few years, and although the management of several companies still rejects the option of distant work, by the advancement of technology it is obvious that the number of employees working from home will grow further. In the EU, 62 percent of employees do part of their work from home, and compared to this, according to a survey those, who cannot use or can only partly use this opportunity, would be willing to sacrifice 20 percent of their salary if they could work from home.

The development of technology not only provides an opportunity for working from home, we can even start an enterprise if we have a good idea.

Be the Buyer[61], recognizing the potential in the technology of the new millennium, developed from a small company into a 100 million dollar business in 10 years. What is the secret of their success? Mostly the exploitation of the opportunities offered by social media, i.e. making friendship circles on social media sites, as the company has done nothing else but asked their followers whether the new pieces of clothes or shoes they would like to sell are good. After processing the answers received, they only start selling goods, which are in accordance with the taste of their followers. However, their success is not only providing good content for consumers and thus made considerate business decisions, but also that they decided to convert to iOS mobiles and tablets among the first.

There are sensible entrepreneurs, who make money by providing entertainment to people so that they are not so lonely. Such an entrepreneur is a lady from South Korea, who provides specific content for users. Park Seo-Yeon[62] realized when she films herself while she is eating and is talking to viewers, they can follow her online, and it can be interesting for many people, mostly young singles. How much Park makes a month from this activity? About 5,000 USD a month, and she only works 3 hours a day. However, for lonely singles this is not the only service provided online. They can even rent a virtual friend for a month for only 25 USD, to send and receive text messages. Already on the first day 5000 people registered for the service, so the creators of Invisible Boyfriend[63] are quite optimistic. When we multiply the number of visitors by 25 dollars each, it becomes apparent what a business loneliness can be.

Of course, big corporations are not left behind, if in this new type of world the aim is to grow the number of consumers. This is well illustrated by the case of a young American woman, who was not hired by a beauty industry giant, Lancôme as a cashier because she had no experience. However, Michelle Phan[64] did not give up, and started a venture online. She uploaded makeup tutorials on YouTube, which were so successful, i.e. had so many viewers within a short time that Lancôme hired her to become the "digital ambassador" of the brand.

NOTES:

1. https://www.theguardian.com/environment/2013/
nov/20/90-companies-man-made-global-warming-emissions-climate-change

2. http://legal-planet.org/2013/09/25/see-stop/

3. http://www.esc.cam.ac.uk/research/research-groups/research-projects/stage-three-project/
stage-three-project-overview

4. https://en.wikipedia.org/wiki/A_Short_History_of_Progress

5. https://qz.com/321248/this-fish-sold-for-37000-at-auction-in-tokyo-two-years-ago-it-
would-have-fetched-1-7-million/

6. http://www.bbc.com/news/science-environment-30934383

7. https://www.information.dk/udland/2013/01/kapitalisme-kritik-helt-ude-skoven

8. http://www.theworldcounts.com/stories/Paper-Waste-Facts

9. http://www.elginrecycling.com/environmental/recycling-facts/

10. http://www.dutchdailynews.com/dutch-office-of-the-future-with-a-ban-on-toilet-paper/

11. http://www.businessinsider.com/
supermarkets-make-you-spend-money-2011-7?op=1#ixzz2GSF7h1lX

12. https://en.wikipedia.org/wiki/Food,_Inc - http://tastethewaste.com/info/film

13. http://tastethewaste.com/info/film

14. https://www.youtube.com/watch?v=NtlvEAe0Ccc

15. https://www.youtube.com/watch?v=65Z21jNQQks - http://www.imperfectproduce.com/

16. http://www.blog.imperfectproduce.com/blog-1/2016/8/8/
happy-birthday-imperfect-a-letter-from-co-founder-and-ceo-ben-simon

17. http://www.zeit.de/politik/ausland/2015-05/lebensmittel-verschwendung-frankreich -
http://www.independent.co.uk/news/world/europe/french-law-bans-supermarkets-throwing-
away-and-spoiling-unsold-food-giving-them-to-food-banks-and-a6855371.html

18. https://www.theguardian.com/world/2015/may/22/
france-to-force-big-supermarkets-to-give-away-unsold-food-to-charity?CMP=fb_gu

19. http://www.nytimes.com/2008/11/29/business/29walmart.html

20. http://www.nbcnews.com/id/27957714/ns/us_news-crime_and_courts/t/dead-after-
shooting-crowded-toys-r-us/#.WL6tC281

21. http://www.economist.com/news/
china/21678008-preparations-are-under-way-orgy-online-spending-bare-and-profligate

22. http://www.economist.com/news/
china/21678008-preparations-are-under-way-orgy-online-spending-bare-and-profligate

23. http://www.bbc.com/capital/story/20150318-tame-your-inner-impulse-buyer

24. http://www.vox.com/2014/8/12/5993075/depression-suicide-13-facts

25. http://www.amazon.com/Positioning-The-Battle-Your-Mind/dp/0071373586

26. https://purelysocial.wordpress.com/2016/03/16/identity-economics/

27. https://www.youtube.com/watch?v=ZmzFZ6KGLSc

28. http://www.the-future-of-commerce.com/2014/11/25/
the-myth-of-the-mansumer-omnichannel-levels-the-shopping-field/

29. https://www.welt.de/wirtschaft/article136738358/Warum-Amazon-jetzt-schonweiss-was-
ich-kaufen-will.html

30. https://www.welt.de/wirtschaft/article136738358/Warum-Amazon-jetzt-schon-weiss-was-
ich-kaufen-will.html

31. http://www.adweek.com/brand-marketing/
american-apparel-files-bankruptcy-protection-167368/

32. http://psychcentral.com/blog/archives/2012/06/02/why-do-women-hate-their-bodies/

33. https://www.ted.com/talks/meaghan_ramsey_why_thinking_you_re_ugly_is_bad_for_you

34. http://www.dailymail.co.uk/femail/article-2029965/Cheryl-Cole-obsession-Charlotte-
ONeill-battles-eating-disorder-star.html

35. https://www.youtube.com/watch?v=XpaOjMXyJGk

36. https://www.youtube.com/watch?v=XpaOjMXyJGk

37. http://www.instyle.com/beauty/15-under-15-best-bargain-beauty-products

38. https://www.youtube.com/watch?v=7WsS27p_wv8

39. https://www.youtube.com/watch?v=xAzK6FK0Gf0

40. http://archive.jsonline.com/business/when-you-gotta-go-toilet-paper-makerditches-the-tube-b99337680z1-272647141.html

41. http://www.hindustantimes.com/gadgets/asus-wants-to-be-a-smartphone-company-not-a-laptop-company/story-UprrXyERKEwmENzpqekFaN.html

42. https://techcrunch.com/2015/02/08/alibaba-meizu/

43.http://www.zdnet.com/article/ces-2015-samsung-internet-of-things/

44. https://dupress.deloitte.com/dup-us-en/industry/retail-distribution/understanding-consumer-behavior-shopping-trends.html

45. http://www.portfolio.hu/short/hamarosan_szu-pertelefonokra_csereljuk_okostelefonjainkat.217916.html?utm_source=index_main&utm_medium=portfolio_box&utm_campaign=portfoliobox

46. https://www2.deloitte.com/global/en/pages/technology-media-and-telecommunications/articles/tmt-pred-contactless-mobile-payments.html

47. https://techcrunch.com/2016/01/28/apple-pay-atm/#.hlrdtid:uazW

48. https://www.youtube.com/watch?v=bnB0yMV90pU

49. http://inforadio.hu/gazdasag/2016/09/15/vege_lesz_az_ertelmetlen_munkak_idoszakanak/

50. http://inforadio.hu/gazdasag/2016/09/15/vege_lesz_az_ertelmetlen_munkak_idoszakanak/

51. http://inforadio.hu/gazdasag/2016/09/15/vege_lesz_az_ertelmetlen_munkak_idoszakanak/

52. http://www.dailymail.co.uk/news/article-3581085/A-robot-teaching-grad-students-5-months-NONE-realized.html

53. https://www.rtinsights.com/production-optimization-real-time-location-system-black-and-decker/

54. https://www.theguardian.com/technology/2016/jun/30/tesla-autopilot-death-self-driving-car-elon-musk

55. http://www.businessinsider.com/report-10-million-self-driving-cars-will-be-on-the-road-by-2020-2015-5-6

56. http://www.reuters.com/article/us-ford-autonomous-idUSKCN10R1G1

57. http://www.theverge.com/2015/6/25/8844649/french-taxi-driver-protest-uber-pop-paris

58. http://www3.weforum.org/docs/WEF_Future_of_Jobs.pdf

59. https://www.forbes.com/sites/laurashin/2016/01/27/work-from-home-in-2016-the-top-100-companies-for-remote-jobs/#5091c5e22741

60. https://www.forbes.com/sites/laurashin/2016/01/27/work-from-home-in-2016-the-top-100-companies-for-remote-jobs/#5091c5e22741

61. http://www.nytimes.com/2013/09/12/fashion/modcloth-is-selling-an-era-they-missed-out-on.html?_r=1

62. http://www.huffingtonpost.com/2014/01/29/eating-in-front-of-webcam-south-korea_n_4686596.html

63. http://mashable.com/2015/01/20/invisible-boyfriend-app-actually-a-thing/

64. http://www.businessinsider.com/

michelle-phans-glam-bags-worth-84-million-2014-10?utm_content=bufferfb1d9

Chapter 3 - Household

,Energy Efficiency: Cheapest Power Around, but Getting More Expensive' GreenTechMedia

THE CITY

Where should we live? - The importance of design in terms of energy use

Household management actually does not begin with leading a household, it starts with an examination of energy and waste management criteria, including the energy consumed in transport, when we choose a house, a flat or, in a word a living space, since the operation of the living space will go together with permanent energy consumption when we live there. It is not indifferent at all how much it will cost, as energy must be paid for all around the world, and, in addition, more and more has had to be paid in recent decades under necessity, maintaining the dependence on providers. It is therefore worth to reflect whether it would be better to find a solution and go off-grid, because if we pay the monthly utility expenses to the provider, we will be deprived of large amounts of money we might as well save.

If we decide to go off-grid, or at least partially detach from the electricity grid, we can build a house with solar panels installed on its roof. In this case we need to make plans and construct properly, otherwise we will do harm to ourselves. If we want to optimally utilize the capacity provided by the roof surface, we will have to build a south-facing house by all means, because this orientation allows the collection of sun rays throughout the day, therefore it generates the most electricity. It is as much as saying not to fall into the trap that we buy a plot, where the local regulations do not allow the optimal placement of the building[1]. Of course, even a house with not an optimal location can collect solar energy via its cells, but obviously not as much as it should, and in this case we would only increase our damage and waste, as we would not generate enough electricity. Subsequently the missing power has to be bought from the provider, which means an expense.

Another example may also highlight the fact how important it is to have a house with low overhead expenses. As opposed to the former example, if we do not build a house, but we buy one, the insulation of the house needs to be taken into account. If the house does not have proper insulation[2], its cooling expense can be up to a considerable amount in summer or even in spring or fall, as in many cases the air conditioning has to be used all day long. In the case of the house having good insulation, no air conditioning expenses will occur, as the inside thermometer will not raise above 77 degrees Fahrenheit, even if the outside temperature is above 95-104 degrees. Thus, we should not spend on cooling the house unnecessarily, if keeping the temperature level can be achieved by other technical solutions, because otherwise, if it is warmer in the living area, extra waste will be produced, the neutralization of which we will have to pay for, too. A house can usually be insulated retrospectively too, the cost of which should be calculated in the purchase of the house, so the desired objective can be achieved, but this should be kept in mind as well. The cost of insulation can also be seen as an investment, because if we do not apply insulation, in a couple of years we will end up paying for cooling in summer and heating in winter, which amounts to the construction costs. We just have to calculate it, or if we fail to do that, energy expert assistance should be sought.

It is an equally important issue how the apartment/house is heated. Burning wood is usually the cheapest option if we operate a Scandinavian stove[3] for this, which heats up to 48 hours[4] with a few loadings and continuously radiates the heat that is inherently more efficient than average stoves. However, they are hardly prevalent in the world, heating is generally solved by natural gas, which is synony-mous with service dependency.

Unfortunately, many people do not take into account energy use when they buy their homes, it is much more important that there is a nearby workplace, a local supermarket, good transport, and a good school for the kids. We must be able to decide what we want. On our part, we would rather provide arguments for planning as thorough-ly as possible, as we will have to pay the utility expenses of the house even if, for example, we retire in 30 years, or in a worse case we get sick, or independently from all this, our job terminates. Consciously thinking people can gather a nice margin over the years, but if they become unemployed for a long term, they may run out of this money.

In many cases, there is simply no possibility to design, as most peo-ple still want to live in cities[5], so they can only buy or rent houses or flats, the energy supply of which has become obsolete. In this case there no other solution than to reduce other expenditures and from this to cover the incurred overheads as much as possible, which can otherwise be comprehended as waste. For instance, we could give up consuming unhealthy foods, as well as we could obtain our fruit and vegetable provision from the countryside to avoid having to pay the reseller benefits. Or preferably, redesigning our lives, we should move to the countryside or to an equally promising garden suburb, where we can establish a much cheaper life if the work can be completed from home. It is never too late. Above all, we should plunge into all of this, when real estate prices are reasonable, for instance, when for the price of an inner-city apartment a detached house with a garden can be bought in the countryside, which is suitable for food production, and some reserve funds will be left in the bank account.

Anyone who is sufficiently far-sighted, would change to energy-saving or even to a passive house, while the latter has not been widespread and formed their market dominance. Indeed, in the 21st century, it will not only be important how much the property is, but how much its operation will be in terms of energy consumption. It the operation cost is zero or just a few dollars a month, everyone will want to move into a passive house, no doubt about it.

Why is it better to live in a city, which is becoming more expensive from year to year?

So many people, so many answers, and it is likely that most of them live there due to their work or family and relatives. It is also possible that the reason for the number of people living there is that they have never asked themselves whether or not it is really better for them to live in the city, comparing the advantages and disadvantages related to cost bearing. In any case, the decades-long trend continues, the world's rural population continues to increasingly move to the cities, where many people do not even realize that life is becoming more expensive every year. According to a list made by Mercer[7], in 2016, Hong Kong is still the first on the list of the most expensive cities, New York is the 11th, London is the 17th, San Francisco and Los Angeles occupy the 27th and the 28th place, and, as the list shows, these cities became even more expensive in 2016, compared to the previous year, except London.

Each city's leadership central task includes energy and food supply, as well as organizing the transportation of the generated waste. It is not difficult to discover the correlation: the more the population is, the more energy and food need to be supplied, while more and more waste mountains need to be transported out of the city, on a daily basis. In terms of financing this means that a city cannot help but become more and more expensive.

Where will this lead to in a finite system?

By 2050, human life will be characterized by steady food, water and energy shortages, as well as accumulated waste mountains the city envisioned as a model, about which a six-part series film was shot by some film makers in 2008, entitled Ecopolis[8]. However, the film makers did not only outline the drawbacks in the series, they also made suggestions on how to create a sustainable city. Although the majority of the suggestions are very resourceful, we find it impossible to create a sustainable city at this stage. Despite being experimented on in several parts of the world, and the film makers also agree that a city could only be sustainable if the energy consumed by the city (input), including food and water supply, could almost immediately be recycled so as not to produce any waste (output). Cities, however, cannot produce this circularity, and no cities or towns in the modern sense will ever be able to do this. Here is a simple example to justify all this. In a survey[9] carried out in Italy in 2011, an environmental protection association examined which are the localities where energy is not lost from buildings due to proper insulation and well-functioning windows. The result shocked the survey makers, as out of the 100 tested public and residential buildings, only Bolzano's buildings passed through the sieve, and in the other cities, a part of the energy immediately ran away due to the poor technical condition of the buildings, i.e. the residents only heated the streets. Since a substantial proportion of energy meant for heating has been lost, with the exception of Bolzano, the inhabitants of the other cities did not produce anything else but waste, thereby losing between EUR 200-500 per year.

Not only heating residential houses, but cooling them is also a significant problem in big cities. According to NASA[10], quarters mostly built of concrete and stone can be up to 1.3 C degrees warmer than those covered by green areas. It is no coincidence that many cities therefore launched Green Roofs[11] programs, such as in New York, in 2013, where the creation of urban gardens on rooftops was promoted. Those who took part in the program received significant tax benefits, thus the city administration was trying to motivate the spreading of natural cooling amid vast amounts of stones. Here is some data concerning a participating garden in the program called Brooklyn Grange[12]: 500 tons of soil is situated on the top of the house built in 1919, but the frame of the building can easily carry it. 40 kinds of plants are grown in 2.5 acres, strictly in a chemical-free way, and the garden provides vegetables for gardeners 9 months a year. In the meantime, it reduces the warming of the building during the hottest summer days by 3-6 degrees[13].

The financial crisis in 2008 and the philosophy of cabin houses

The financial crisis in 2008 made a lot of people realize that their way of life was too costly, absolutely unsustainable, and that they should live in a different way. Some of them were forced to change since they had lost almost all their properties, houses, cars, and tangible assets. Their ambivalent feelings and anger because of the situation is well summarized by Dee Williams, builder of one of the cabin houses, who wrote about it in The Big Tiny. In his book entitled Built-

It-Myself Memoir[14], he writes about it like this: 'What if I sold my big house with its rats in the front yard, the mortgage, the hours of dusting, mopping, cleaning, vacuuming, painting, grass cutting, and yard pruning? How would it feel to live so easily?'

As cabin houses meant a solution for many people to restart their lives after the economic recession, it was a huge success in the US, and it started its journey of conquest throughout the world. Since the floor-space of a cabin house is not more than 300 ft^2, its operation obviously consumes much less expense than a house William used to live in. Of course, anyone may raise the question of how it is possible to live in such a little hut, on such a tiny floor-space. The opinions of the new owners are all the same, they love these houses and find them homely, especially if they build them themselves. If the house is also mobile, it makes it possible for the owner to wander around the whole country, enjoying a lot of freedom, as no accommodation fee has to be paid anywhere. Alexis Stephens and Christian Parson did so too in 2015, and travelled around America. Daily Mail[15] reported on their 18-month-long journey as a very interesting initiative, however, they documented how it is possible to live in a cabin house themselves, too. Their lifestyle can be said to be puritan and economizing, which is illustrated on their website[16]. As it can be seen, there are no useless tools, everything has its functionality. The couple wrote about their experiences gained along the way on their blog, but you can continuously listen to their radio program[17], and a film was shot about their expedition[18] to show how it is possible to give up the traditional lifestyle and live in a sustainable way and live well at the same time.

All of a sudden, there was such a big demand to purchase these houses that the success of cabin houses urged some designers to plan the prototype of a cabin house and start its production. For example, the picture shows a nice looking little house built by the Dutch cabinet-maker Dimka Wintzel[19], with the help of Walden Studio. Conforming to regulations and provided with every license for housing, the 183-ft² floor area mobile house is equipped with solar panels and a wood-burning fireplace, and in addition, an interposed specific filter collects the rain water, and besides the basic equipment, a shower and a septic compost toilet are also available upon request.

The hut's greatness lies in its equipment and self-sufficiency in terms of energy resources, and more. Owing to its low cost, as opposed to traditional houses, no mortgage tax can be imposed on cabin houses as an extra expense, it is independent from multinational energy providers making their customers pay for energy provision, and if we set it up in a place where our self-sufficiency can be partially solved by growing vegetables and fruits, we will not have to purchase increasingly expensive foods in supermarkets for decades. We do not have to pay the merchants' profit at all. All this, however, does not end here, the listed facts can be supplemented by two more. For the very reason that the Wintzel kind of cabin house does not or hardly produces waste, it is much cheaper than any conventional dwelling. As a result, its inhabitant can easily survive a crisis like in 2008, which ruined the life of Dee Williams.

Of course, by giving these examples we do not want anyone to abandon their current way of life and move into a cabin house. We wanted to present that life can be much less costly in a house with a smaller floor space, compared to houses or flats where people usually live in welfare societies.

Eco parks and sustainable settlements of the future

Self-sufficiency, the concept of the minimum necessary energy intake and little or no waste production prompted engineers to design and set for the construction of self-sufficient minor districts, commonly known as eco parks, showing how the flaws of cities built 100-150 years ago can be eliminated. In the beginning of the century, the Swedes built a district consisting of such residential and office buildings in Malmö[20], in the place of a completely rundown port area, which had practically become waste. In compliance with modern condominium policies, it is based on integrated energy resources, i.e. it combines alternative energy resources, so it is multifaceted. Electricity is mostly generated by wind turbines and solar panels, but geothermal energy is also utilized. Several houses have a 154-ton shade giving 'solar hat', which makes the overheating of buildings impossible in summer, so little power is needed to waste on the operation of air conditioners. In apartment buildings, power is mostly needed for lighting and to operate electronic devices, as well as to supply the energy-guzzling office buildings, including the Turning Torso building. Winters in Sweden are quite severe, so obviously geothermal energy provides heating, which is given in many places in the Nordic countries. Selective waste collection is completely solved in the locality, and nothing is lost from organic kitchen waste, as biofuels are produced from it. The quarter's carbon dioxide emission is optimal, because the locality's 'legal regulation' simply bans cars from the streets. Each family is allowed to use only 0.6 unit of car.

The eco quarter, which, in terms of waste management, means a major step forward compared to former traditional urban parts, naturally did not establish for food production, however, new projects have emerged in the last few years, which aim to settle it within the city. The main reason for this is large-scale agriculture, which goes together with increasing water consumption and deforestation, as well as destroys the topsoil of the land, and, in addition, not only the land and the environment, but also the rivers and lakes are loaded with chemicals. If humanity does not want to starve due to the desolation of topsoil, a change is needed, and the vast majority of food should be produced locally. In accordance with this concept and according to the plan, the first green village has started to be built in the outskirts of a city called Almere, which abandons large-scale agriculture food supply, and it would be self-sufficient in all respects, its vertical farms would provide food and energy supply, and, in addition, this self-sustaining locality would not produce waste. According to James Ehrlich, CEO of ReGen Villages[21], Californian project company, 'we are redefining residential real-estate development by creating these regenerative neighborhoods'. It is not only about redefining real-estate development, but also city development, as illustrated by the drawings[22] and photos of the plan. What will the dwelling-houses be like in reality?

We will find out about it in 2017, as the provision of the first few houses will take place then. After a few years of operation it will become clear whether or not it is financially worth developing such villages and establishing family life there.

If it is not yet worth it, we should not despair, as we still have the example of the Dervaes[23] family concerning how to purchase a detached house with a garden to be restored, therefore at a cheap price, and then how to manage farming there, just like our ancestors did 100-150 years ago. Purchasing such a house requires little investment, it can be completely restored or developed later, while it will provide food in abundance that is we can conduct a lifestyle by which we may become mostly independent from energy providers, and in the case of a crisis we may be able to survive a difficult period.

Although we could see in connection with the Swedish, half-Dutch and half-American model how companies and individuals imagine the development of a sustainable city, we must not forget that the process is much easier if it is enhanced by political decision-makers as well. In 2013, the EU imposed a binding regulation on the member countries, according to which only passive, more precisely zero-energy consumption houses can be built in the territory of the Union, starting from 2020, including major restauration, too.

Energy and energy consumption

While technical devices are getting better and cheaper, by which daily energy use may be more effective and cheaper - for instance, most recently MIT[24] has come up with a revolutionary development, informing that solar panels can generate electric power even in darkness (this should be checked more thoroughly to see whether it is so) - professionals in environmental protection and energy efficiency agree that the optimal use of energy does not depend on the development level of devices, but on changing human behavior. Average citizens do not even realize how lavishing lifestyle they conduct or their energy consumption is, and if they lived in a more economizing way than previously by learning proper behaviors, they could save a lot more money than they would think. Doing so would be better for them and would do good to the environment as well.

Power consumption

In Japan, in the framework of a project[25] it was examined how the operation of an office building could be transformed in order to use less power than before, and how the people working there would be able to adapt to this. Although the office building already had traditional devices suitable for green energy use, additional green devices would be built into the corridor floors, utilizing vibrational energy from walking on the floors and contributing to the generation of the daily power volume. The workers walking along the specific sections of the corridor steadily produced power during worktime. Many people would smile to see the sight of workers walking all in a row, but if we consider how many frequented places in a city are suitable to utilize the vibrational energy of the crowds, then it would seem a challenging initiative, especially if we also watch the short video about the subject[26]. Not only this strange behavior is obligatory in the office building, there are some other regulations, too. Meeting time is strictly scheduled for one hour, so when one hour has passed, the lights go out in the meeting rooms, the meeting is interrupted, which makes the participants finish any discussion in one hour. This solution might also seem weird, just like the sight of the people circulating on a specific passage, however, it is really surprising that 20% of the energy consumption of the office building is covered by changing behaviors.

What we can accomplish is just a few examples of the many

Before illustrating by some examples how we economize on electricity like the Japanese, it is worth to note what we should start with when we have decided to save energy, including electricity. Browsing through the intended websites of providers and green organizations, we can gather complete knowledge about what we can utilize from what we have read there, and what we cannot, as customs vary. In addition, there might occur some tips among the many we have never thought of, even though a lot of money could have been saved by utilizing them. I remember the solar energy oven was one of them, which, if set up in the garden, is suitable for preparing a variety of dishes. Jan Bohmer made the so-called Kyoto box[27] appliance from cheap parts worth of 5 dollars in Kenya to help those in Africa living in the open air, without electric power, and at the same time cutting wood to consume in fire, which helps the desertification process. When we consider how many hundreds of millions or billions of people are still living in Stone Age environment in Africa or Asia, it is easy to imagine the significance of Bohmer's invention for saving trees and the environment. In 2009, the inventor's oven won a Climate Change Challenge award of the Financial Times, which is a simple device we could also use if we want to save electricity, just like the often-mentioned Dervaes family.

The Japanese examples are interesting because they show the patterns of behavior we can also learn, however, there are patterns, which are obviously can hardly be followed if at all. Actually, anyone can decide how far to go in changing their habits, and this does not require an objective limiting factor such as the automatic turning off the lights in the Japanese example. We can voluntarily decide when to read or work, either during the daytime, when these activities do not need lighting, or in the evening. Apart from our housekeeping, we can encounter limiting factors, such as a hand dryer in a supermarket washroom, which works only for a few seconds and then it turns off. Operating a hand dryer in our home does not seem to be a very smart choice, as we can use our own towel, which does not consume electric power, however, in many households, the washroom could bear an automatically operating IR-aware tap, which only briefly lets the water, just long enough to quickly wash our hands. Many of us are able to let the water flow in our homes for hours when shaving, for example, which can waste large quantities of water.

If we want to economize on electric power for a lifetime, we should also transform our technical device related shopping habits, so it is advisable to buy or change to household appliances, for example, a dishwasher or a washing machine, a fridge or a deep-freezing refrigerator, as well as light bulbs[28], which are more expensive, however they are worth their price, as during operation they will prove to be remunerative sooner or later. Posts concerning these appliances and 'who would sell what' often appear on social networking sites, on Facebook, for instance, and it does not do any harm to watch them, because many devices can be bought at much cheaper prices, even if they are a bit used. Free ads can also be posted about what we are looking for, so we can speed up the process. Of course, it is advisable to make professional posts, using the most impressive photos, otherwise nobody will click on our ad and therefore the ad will become waste. In connection with household items, it is important to highlight that we should borrow what we can instead of buying them.

For example, if a drill is only used once or twice, it is sure that we will not need it later, so it will be added to a series of objects with no function, and if we want to sell it, we will barely get anything for it. It could also be exchanged or occasionally rented out[29] if possible, however, it is the best not to buy it.

Some of the household appliances can be used by a community. E.g. if the resident community buys three washing machines, and the washing for 50 resident families is done in a room established for this purpose, the residents can save significant amount of money, as the household device does not have to be bought by each family[30]. Naturally, a kind of 'timetable' needs to be developed, but the idea certainly works well. Almost the same principle applies to food or usually lunch sharing, but only if the related service is available at our living place. If we want to buy delicious food from reliable sources, we do not have to do anything else just register on the homepage[31], which registers where we can buy our favorite food on a daily basis. When we have ordered the dish where it was made, we can have it on the spot. It is a more environmentally friendly solution, but if we want to take it away, then wrapping is also needed. The wrapping will be thrown away later if we do not use the same box, so unfortunately, we cannot help producing waste.

Lunch, however, cannot only be taken from individuals. It is already working in Denmark, and To Good To Go[32] service has recently been introduced
in England, whose website if we register on, we will learn from when and for how much we can buy the food left over from lunch at different restaurants. Compared to standard prices, the absolutely consumable remains are much cheaper and usually abundant, so with regular consumption we can decrease our expenses, and, by the way, the cooking does not consume power and it does not take our time if we have little. As the saying goes, the day only has 24 hours.

Of course, we should only use the services if we cannot prepare our own lunch or adapt our lives to be able to 'waste' the necessary time on ourselves. It obvious that the cheapest food is always what we prepare ourselves. From the viewpoint of our health, the time spent on it and the amount paid for electricity are subsidiary issues if we prepare our own dishes.

There are other ways to save significant amounts spent on electricity, too. In many homes, it would also have a good result to power down the 'vegetating' devices in online operating mode[33], especially gaming consoles, computers since a lot of money could be saved by considering and applying the principle of 'it is the numbers that pay', as it was described in Chapter 1. At the level of the American society, up to 80 billion dollars could be saved, which could rise to 120 dollars by 2020, if we buy more of these devices. And more of them will be bought, no doubt about it.

In connection with cabin houses, it was already explained why it was important to live in a smaller space from the point of view of optimal energy consumption. In other words, we should never be in two rooms at the same time, so we might want to buy a flat or a house, or typically rent one in a city, which is just enough spacious for us and family members. Decision making is not easy sometimes, but knowing the habits of the family members we can estimate the living-space needed to live conflict-free, yet in an energy efficient way. A number of videos or series of photos are about how to make best use of space. A young couple in Kiev lives in an apartment[34] that is only 322 ft². If we have a look at the photos taken of the flat, there are two striking things at once. Every part of the space has its functionality, it is fully inhabited, so the energy supply should also be focused on one room, not two or more. The other thing is that there are no unnecessary things without a function. The space can also be filled in by smart-furniture in the apartment, for example, as shown in the Dezeen Magazine[35] video, where the bed slides under the cabinet, and the cabinet can be also be moved back and forth in case the center space needs to be greater or smaller. Even though smart devices operate with electricity, they consume less power if we live in a smaller space instead of a bigger flat with many rooms or a house.

More and more money should be paid for electricity

It is a tendency in every country that more and more should be paid for power supply, as the graph shows it in the case of the US, since 2001[36]. Of course, sometimes there are refreshing exceptions, such as Cost Rica[37]. However, the number of domestic power plant set up tends to grow along with lowering the prices of solar panels and increasing their efficiency. Therefore, if possible, it is recommended to purchase a house or move into a house, which already has solar panels or they can be mounted on its roof. It would not be difficult Rettenbach[38], a little village close to Munich, having almost 1500 inhabitants, as solar cell can be seen on almost every roof of public buildings and houses, proclaiming that all the residents of the locality are green. However, Germany has not only appeared in the news because of this small village in recent years. The German Government was puzzled at the nuclear disaster of Fukushima, which resulted in a decision to close down all nuclear power plants within a few years and switch to green energy. The experience shows that in spite of the resulted contradictions, it is still worth it. Most recently, the fact that consumers suddenly generated too much green power caused a major problem[39], as it could not be sustained in the conventional grid. Namely, if the system is overloaded, it will result in wastage, generating great losses, as the consumers have not produced anything else but waste. We may wonder why the providers did not generate less power at the same time, just enough to balance the system. Unfortunately, the system is not yet prepared for this, it was not designed and continuously developed for this, and it should be transformed accordingly in the coming years. However, from the consumers' point of view, the real problem is not caused by the domestic power plant's generating too much power, but the other way around. If there are fewer hours of sunshine, there will be less power, too. For this reason, the provider needs power supply, against which the only way of 'defense' is what the Dervaes family does. They utilize alternative lighting devices used by our great-grandmothers, who still lived their daily lives without electricity. By forming their appropriate habits, the family living in Pasadena could almost create a real balance between their power consumption and generation, so it happened that they only had to pay 12 dollars to the provider in a year. We believe that this amount can be covered from their income of 200,000 dollars resulting from their being self-sufficient, as they mostly sell foods, fruits, and vegetables.

When will all of us generate electricity for ourselves? It is not known yet. Presumably, there will always be and remain providers, however, their role and dominance can significantly be reduced. The tendency of how big the power business, and, in wider sense energy provision can be until reaching the idyllic condition is shown by the fact that in 2016 the Rockefeller family[40] withdrew or seemed to have withdrawn from energy production based on hydrocarbons, and, as others[41] had previously done, they made investments into green energy production. Even in the family referred to their responsibility for global warming and moral reasons concerning their decision-making, still there were hard-core business interests in the background, as more and more investors, such as the pension insurance funds handling enormous fortunes, would start withdrawing their invested money from businesses deemed risky. Especially after a number of countries ratified the Paris Climate Convention in 2015, even China and the USA, in 2016.

Community Power Supply

A community can produce the food for themselves, and similarly generate the electric power needed, or a part of it. Even a smaller solar park can be operated for this purpose. Such a settlement is Burlington[42] in the US, Vermont State. The town with 42,000 inhabitants would like to save 20 million dollars with green energy resources in the next 10 years. Not only Americans are foregoers of solar energy utilization. For instance, cooperation with a provider can also be developed, which may terminate dependency in a traditional sense. Since 2012, the Austrian Wien Energie[43] has established 25 community power plants with residential financing. Since then they have provided 800,000 people with green electricity, and their goal is to double this number by 2030. Their success lies in the strength of unity in the community, as evidenced by the fact that six thousand people have purchased shares in the company so far. The example may be inspiring if the conditions are given, and similar solutions can be introduced anywhere in the world. The Austrians do not only trust the power of their community, but also their own knowledge. They have already started to develop the smart city in Aspern, which collects data on the energy use of buildings already completed so that researchers can design future buildings to be much more energy efficient. During data collection even the heat loss deriving from the residents' switching on and off the lights is measured. Why is it interesting? If this energy is not lost in the future, the city will not produce 'waste' either, which allows for the most optimal energy utilization[44].

Some Tips

1. General knowledge: If we primarily want to economize, the best option is to study several websites dealing with electric power savings. As a matter of fact, a whole literature can be found on the Internet, so we can get to know some we would never think of in our lives and would never use. In this case, we would consume energy in a way that we would never realize how much energy is wasted in reality. Such waste production is to be avoided.

2. Energy-efficient Lighting: It has been described above why LED lighting is better. On the website cnet.com[45], we can thoroughly examine why it is worth switching to LED lighting and how much energy can be saved over a given period. Based on this, anyone can calculate how much money can be saved within a year. Our calculations showed that with the use of LED, the returns on investment in the case of cheaper products was half a year, while in the case of more expensive ones it was one year. During our calculation a 60-Watt bulb was changed to a 9-Watt LED bulb, with which 7 dollars could be saved in one year, if we considered that the bulb operated 1,000 hours. Depending on how many LED bulbs we have in our flat or house and how long they operate, quite nice savings can be achieved annually.

3. Household appliances: We should give priority to household appliances that are energy efficient. Although they are more expensive than conventional appliances, they will be remunerative after a certain time. This can be calculated. Planned obsolescence and the service demand of the respective item should also be considered, otherwise it will come off badly. To avoid this, not only the product tests should be read through, but we need to check what forums have been published about the respective product.

In connection with some devices, however, we should think over if we really need the product. For example, it is not sure that a spin-drier is needed if we can dry our clothes in the Sun or on a drying rack. Traders also sell countless devices, which are not needed at all. Just think of electric bread slicers and power operated corkscrews. We should not buy these devices, not only because they are not needed from the outset, but also because they will break down and become nothing else but useless junk that is waste.

It may also be in question whether we should iron all our clothes or fabrics. For example, bedsheets and pillowcases can be used whether they are ironed or not. (More detailed description can be found about the shirt that can be worn several times throughout the year without washing or ironing in the section about washing.)

We should place our fridge in the kitchen, clean and defrost is according to the instructions for use.

4. Regrouping and transformation of habits: The tasks that can also be done during the day should be regrouped so as to avoid light-ing, because the best energy is the unconsumed energy. Guided by this principle, we can conduct a more organized life, such as when teleworking, we can use Hoffice services. When ten people are work-ing in one person's apartment in summer, and the air conditioning must be operated because of the heat, nine of them surely will not use their own appliance.

Anyway, we need to pay attention when and how we can econ-omize with our appliances using electric power. Proper behavior-al patterns should be applied for this, which will become automatic after a while, so the new patterns will soon stabilize. All this should be taught to our children as well.

5. Stand-by Mode: The devices needlessly consuming electric power should be unplugged if we do not use them. For this reason, biased toggle switch adapters can be purchased to switch off all our devices, such as the TV-set, game consoles, and CD player, etc.

6. Cooking[46] can be much more energy efficient than we think. For example, when we prepare food in oven, it can be switched off in the last 10 minutes, as there will be enough heat to finish the preparing process. In connection with this example we should search for sites on the Internet that will provide additional examples of how to economize with technologies for certain cooking or baking processes. These technologies are not only good for saving electric power, but economizing with other resources, such as water. For example, if we do not add four times as much water to the pasta as described in some recipe books, just the quantity enough to cover the pasta, and we stir it while cooking to avoid sticking together, we can save up to one hundred liters of water in one year. Anyway, many people drink the cooking water too, especially if it is dredged with organic seasoning. The same is applicable in the case of cooking potatoes.

HEATING

It is evident that the space we live in has to be provided with electricity and heated in winter. However, it is not indifferent what we use for heating. Iceand's[47] residents are lucky, because unlimited geothermal energy is available on the island, so its inhabitants hardly have to pay for heating and hot water, the heat of the Earth is an unlimited resource. The heat is not only used to operate their houses, but also their greenhouses in which vegetables are grown, so to speak, they live well in terms of energy supply, independently from other countries. If a special technology was available, their cars would also be operated by hot water, but lacking this technology they also have to pay for oil, so in this respect they are also dependent on countries from which they import oil. Unlike in Iceland, in many other countries around the world heating provided by providers must be paid for, where heating typically happens by burning natural gas, oil or coal[48].

Heating is becoming more and more expensive in the world

If we consider energy supply in the past few decades, it is absolutely clear that the use of hydrocarbons for heating as well as electric supply is becoming more expensive all around the world. Despite the fact that more and more people are investing into green energy, it can only be concluded that oil-based societies will certainly remain until 2050, and oil lobby will still be present and prevail, even if its rate gradually declines. Obviously, we will or would have to finance the presence of the oil lobby, as expected. It will happen so if we allow.

The shock that the price of oil would keep rising reached oil-based societies in the '70s, most notably the US and Europe, when the Arab States started to raise oil prices. In a sudden lack of supply in the US, people started to fight over fuel at gas stations, and chaos emerged at many places in the country within a few days. At that time, many people became aware that energy would just keep getting more expensive in the coming decades, therefore it would be worth looking for alternative solutions allowing the detachment from the oil-based society, even if we have to live in it.

We do not necessarily think of a change done by the Hejlskov family in Denmark[49] much later, in 2011, however, their exodus from civilization is thought-provoking. Having had enough of more and more outstanding invoices and having to work more and more, Andrea Hejlskov and family moved to a forest in Sweden to escape modern slavery and to be able to finance their way of life. They built their wooden house there, which had no electricity, central heating, water, not even Internet in the first year, yet there they began a new life with their children with no intention of returning to the city.

Although the anti-capitalist philosophy of the Danish family, their dim view of welfare society and completely going off-grid is very appealing, we still think that there is no need to completely withdraw from society, and the dependence on oil-based society can be eliminated or limited in other ways. Actually, we need to live in the way our great-grandmothers did, when almost no one knew how precious treasure hydrocarbons were, what a big power and profit they would provide to those who would manufacture products from it and sell them to 'people in need'. Typically, about 130 years ago heating had been resolved with wood or coal everywhere, natural gas became dominant in developed countries only after that, displacing wood as a reproducible resource in a few years or decades without any problem. Reproduction can be done locally, under sustainable forest management. But now, in addition to oil, natural gas is also getting increasingly more expensive on the world market, and the role of wood is rising again.

If we live in any of the cities, there is no way to find a flat, with honorable exceptions, where there is no gas introduced, or where heating can be done with wood, although there still may be some exceptions. The same as is typical of villages as well, but still we can find some houses, where heating can be solved in a hybrid[50] way, i.e. with natural gas and wood.

A total separation from natural gas, however, is an illusion in many cases, because the heat needed for cooking and baking can almost entirely be produced by this kind of energy. Naturally, warm water can also be obtained from solar collectors, or if we have solar cells, electric power needed for food production can also be generated by these technical devices, however, they are not yet as widespread in every country as they should be.

Those who live in a city and pay a lot for heating should not renounce reducing their bills either. On the one hand, regrouping can be done by economizing on costs to cover heating expenses, and, on the other hand, personal habits can also be transformed to save on bills.

Which are the most important?

1. Acquiring Information: It is worth beginning with studying the national or local websites operated by providers or green organiza-

tions that may give Tips on how to save on heating in our environment. It is important for the very reason that we may read about technical solutions and behavioral patterns, which otherwise would never come to mind, though a lot can be saved by their use.

2. Temperature Control in General: Unfortunately, a lot of people go out to work leaving the heating on, so the apartment is using energy even when they are not at home. It is a form of neglect, improper behavior, just like when others do not de-energize 'vegetating' devices in online mode. Compared to reckless behavior, it is even more severe if we do not turn off the heating, because we would like to be received by the same warm temperature as it was when we left for work. In this case, the fact that the apartment will now cool down completely during the day, as it would take longer than our time spent at work, and when we return, the flat can soon be re-heated, just in 30 minutes.

Automatic Thermostat: In case we are not at home or a lower inside temperature is sufficient at night, a programmable thermostat may come in handy, which does not constitute a major investment. It automatically adjusts the temperature and provides the necessary constant temperature in the house or flat. This is especially for those who tend to forget about turning the heating up or down, or they are accustomed to convenience.

3. Temperature Control Individually: When at home, we can test how our body responds to turning the heating down by one or two degrees. If it does not cause any particular problem, we can do this for a longer period so as to reduce our bills. It may result in a lot of savings over the years, because we all know that it is the numbers that pay. We can turn down the heating even more, especially if we wear thicker clothes. Polar outfits made of PET bottles from second hand shops can do wonders for many years, especially when you watch TV or sit in

front of your computer without moving for a longer time, i.e. the body does not produce enough own heat. Of course, everyone should go as far in changing their own habits and behaviors as they can stand. As a result of work, constantly tired city-dwellers, who usually get cold twice a year, could easily get sick, except if getting tired, fatigue and flu diseases are balanced with an appropriate lifestyle, especially being on a proper diet, i.e. that keep the immune system at an appropriate level, but that is another story. Not only during the day, the inside temperature can be reduced at night, especially if our blankets or quilts already provide adequate warmth. Anyway, the aim is that we should provide the necessary body heat to achieve a perfect sleep, and the cover should only trap the heat, so that we should not be heated beyond by the environment, as human organism cannot rest in excessive heat. Since heating dries the air, the lost humidity has to be compensated, because it influences the sleeping process and the development of illnesses. There is no uniform recipe for setting the heating to a certain degree, what to wear during the day, and what blanket or pajamas to use at night, so everyone should find the optimal solution.

Insulation: An Italian survey concerning Bolzano highlighted how important the quality of doors and windows is, with no gap closing, as the amount equaled up to EUR 200-500 that was yearly lost by heating the streets in Italy. The problem is not unique. A mass of old building or houses[51] can be found in America, the UK, and anywhere in the world, the doors and windows of which are completely obsolete and are in the need of exchange or at least proper insulation, but this work is carried out by few people. In many cases, it would be a result to place decorative or funny cushions or textiles[52] between the windowpanes if possible, or in front of the windows or doors as draft shields, so that the heat will not escape. Unfortunately, only a few make use of this option. Although this solution is to temporarily reduce waste, obviously the goal is to definitely abolish energy losses caused by draft. There is no wizardry in it, as it can also be seen in the video[53], anyone can perform the given task. It does not require anything else, just a few dollars investment, in exchange for hundreds saved a year.

The best solution, however, is to modernize not only the doors and windows, but to insulate the whole house if the financial conditions are provided for this. This solution can be perceived as a kind of investment, as it is possible to calculate how long it will take to pay for itself. In addition, the operation, as shown in the video[54], is not as complicated as it seems.

5. Hoffice: The digital revolution and the community share-based economy can also help to reduce our heating expenses. Our apartment can be shared with others for work purposes during the day, while we are working at our workplaces, and we also join in such a community if we perform telework, however, after a while we would be inspired in our lonely and dull homes by the community. In any case, only one apartment should be heated, and in addition, other cost can be shared in the community, so we can calculate whether or not it is worth working in someone else's apartment. The spread of the movement proves that it is worth it, however, it should be added immediately that the emergence of Hoffice[55] was not only due to sharing costs, but rather to the fact that people tried to avoid working alone at home and preferring work in a real community, taking advantage of all its benefits. Of course, if we put our apartment at others' disposal, our vegetating living space will be transformed into a lucrative property, which will increase our monthly income in all ways, while if we join in such a community, we can significantly decrease our overhead expenses, including the heating bills.

6. Credit Exchange: Banks will come up with newer and newer products on the market, so we can also study them at times whether we could change our previous credit for restauration and the reconstruction of the heating system to a new credit with cheaper repayments. It is applicable in the case when we explicitly took out the loan to be able to save money with more modern appliances. In this case, we might as well cover the repayments with the saved amount or a part of it.

Everything is cheaper in the countryside

Although heating can also be optimized and costs can be reduced in a city apartment, this does not change the fact that heating, just like any other energy resources, is becoming increasingly expensive. This shows a tendency that it is rewarding to change and move to the countryside, if we have not used the option yet. Otherwise, in this respect, it is all the same whether to move to a small village or to the outskirts of a city. The point is to be able to create our own lives, which is independent from service providers. We can be motivated by something else, too. After having lived in the city for 25 years, when I myself decided to move out of it, I had three main reasons in mind to explain my decision to my partner. Country life is generally cheaper, and we can produce and consume healthy food instead of consuming products found in supermarkets, yet real estate purchase and its operation regarding energy consumption consumes little money. In other words, if we live in a city, we mostly produce money for service providers and traders, not for ourselves, and this means a kind of addictive modern-day slavery, which is absolutely unnecessary. Moreover, if we perceive this as a process, we can consider ourselves lucky if we have not caught some sort of more serious civilization disease, such as high blood pressure, obesity, cancer, just to mention three of them.

We could also say that urban life is nothing else but an accumulation of deficit, paying unnecessary costs and expenses, which are actually nothing more than a steady production of waste.

When we had moved to the countryside in the spring of 2016, and having lived there for the first 6 months, we had enough time to actually compare the costs on which we could significantly economize. Of course, these expenses included the heating bill, which, according to our expectations, showed a significant difference in rates in favor of the countryside. In May, we ordered and paid for the firewood, as its market allows pretty good bargaining then. Listening to the previous owner's advice, we ordered 40 tons of wood, which had to be enough to keep our house warm all through the winter and partly in spring as well. For this we paid 215 dollars, which was approximately half of the amount we had had to pay for heating a 645-ft² flat in the city.

Before ordering firewood, however, we had checked the materials related to wood heating on the net to avoid unnecessary waste production. Actually, many people think that the wood only has to be bought, cut to proper size and put on the fire, and from that point everything will work automatically. This is of course not that easy.

Firewood must be used optimally

First of all, we should get at least two years old, appropriate firewood for proper burning, which is really dry, otherwise 40 percent of the wood and therefore the produced heat would be wasted, so we would produce nothing else but waste in almost half-and-half proportion.

For optimal burning, it is worth watching the video about how to burn correctly in your wood stove[56], as well as the videos about the use of a rocket stove[57] or a rocket mass heater[58].

WATER CONSUMPTION

What do Cameron Diaz and Jennifer Aniston have in common? Well, not just that they both are American actresses, but also something else. Unlike average consumers, they both are aware that water is a scarce resource, therefore they significantly economize on it at home, setting a good example as to how to optimally use the running resource by changing our habits. For example, Aniston[59] takes no more than three-minute-long showers and also includes tooth-brushing, while Cameron Diaz[60] flushes the toilet only after the second pee. This might not seem such a big performance, but if we consider that toilet flushing[61] in itself makes up one third of water consumption in welfare societies, we might guess the quantity it involves. Only in England, 720 million liters of water could be saved per year if everyone peed in the shower, as suggested by two English students[62], who, besides the excessive water consumption, wanted to draw the attention to the essence of real savings that lies in changing our habits and therefore our way of thinking related to the issue, and not just buying better and more efficient appliances, which is only half the battle. But let's just have a look at the numbers. A toilet flushing uses approx. 1 gallon of water, which means about 3,650 gallons of water a year. A gallon of water costs USD 0.03, therefore it will cost USD 10,95 by the end of the year. According to some statistics, a person flushes the toilet five times a day on average, depending on whether it is about number one or number two. If the collecting method[63] is applied, i.e. if we do not flush the toilet each time after peeing, the number of flushes can be reduced to two or three. Obviously, we can save money in the same proportion, especially when we consider that many a little makes a mickle.

It does not sound much, does it? However, we do not flush the toilet only once a day, in fact... in the case of a family of five, each member does that five times a day, which comes to 25 times... We still can reduce the expenses a little by changing our habits. Ideally, it can be presumed that this can be carried out within a period of time, for instance, from 6 a.m. to 8 a.m., so the quantity of water would be closer to the value arisen in the context of one person's consumption. Naturally, this is not easy at a workplace where up to 50 people use the same toilet in the same period of time, it is simply impractical. So, it is almost certain that lavishness will remain for some time, until composting toilets will be made regular, which recycle all humanure.

Until we have composting toilets at our workplaces and homes, we can only economize by changing our habits. The question is how far we can go in this process. There are some conscious people, who hardly spend on flushing the toilet. With a simple but effective method, water used for hand-washing can be accumulated in a bucket, which can later be used for flushing the toilet. In fact, there are people who occasionally fit the pipe of the washing machine into the bucket to accumulate the grey water and flush the toilet after having mopped up the kitchen or other parts of the apartment with it.

Naturally, the composting toilet[64] would be the simplest and most convenient solution, without the use of any water, even if we go to do the number two. A composting toilet either set up in our garden with our own hands or we operate another company product in our bathroom, it does not require water use, no matter how surprising it may sound to many. Both are able to recycle human feces, whereby the material returns to the place where it comes from, i.e. to nature. With an annual quantity, half of the nutritional requirements of the arable land used for one person could be recycled, while the other half would come from the vegetable waste[65] generated there, so our food production could become sustainable if this solution prevailed in practice. Unfortunately, large-scale agriculture is accepted everywhere nowadays, so the fertilizer will not be replaced, in fact, it is neutralized in a system that requires the use of an excess of additional energy, not to mention that its construction is very expensive, too. It is not yet known when canals and wastewater treatment plants will close to be replaced by a system based on a sustainable processing cycle. However, it should be in demand, as according to some calculations, our arable lands will completely be exhausted within a few decades. According to John Crawford[66], head of Sustainable Agricultural Department of the University of Sydney, soil degradation compared to natural recovery pace is 57 times faster in China, 17 time faster in Europe, 10 times faster in America, and 5 times faster in Australia, so 80 percent of the world's arable land is already or moderately eroded.

Anyone may raise the question whether composting toilets stink or not. Everybody can be reassured that they do not stink, or it smells just like any other toilet use, which will only last until it is flushed. However, in the case of conventional use, we should avoid accumulating it together with the urine, as it will have a significant odor impact. Consideration should be given, as family members used to traditional lifestyle will find it more inconvenient to change, in fact, some of them will be stubbornly resistant, so they should be moderately introduced to the world of savings, otherwise they will never cooperate with us. They have become so addicted to their background and ingrained habits that it can be difficult to persuade them to follow simpler and more common solutions, such as selective waste gathering or not to buy unnecessary things.

At the beginning of this chapter it has been mentioned how important to consider energy consumption and making thorough plans are before purchasing a house if we want to provide our living space with an optimal energy supply, such as generating electric power for ourselves. The same applies to water use as well, because if inappropriate or obsolete appliances are operated in the bathroom, a lot of money will be lost over the years, as some of the water will trickle down the drain without meaningful use. Future households will certainly have bathrooms or toilets, which will inherently economize on water, so easy-going consumers will just need to have it built into the house, however, the vast majority of today's cities operate outdated technology, therefore everyone should individually decide how to live in a more economizing way. Rethinking and testing this is a long process, as new ideas will flash through one's mind, and some devices will be changed, such as a faucet or a toilet bowl, if needed. At the beginning of this process, it is worth visiting the manufacturers' websites and consulting an advisor, who practically knows which company's product should be preferred. What we ourselves can do is listed below:

1. Although the consequence of letting the water flow unnecessarily is well-known, still, unfortunately, this is the practice in many households. Water is flowing when men shave their faces and women shave their legs, and also when they brush their teeth. In the latter case, it is recommended to buy tumblers, which will not only be good, because the will not be flowing while tooth-brushing, but also because, seeing this, the Pavlovian reflex will be fixated to avoid wasting water. Finally we will get to the level that we do not even notice that we automatically save water. We can also plug the sink when shaving or ladies can use a vessel for this purpose. Similarly, we should also economize when washing hands or faces, as an average consumer unnecessarily flows the water while doing it. In this case, it can also be a solution to pour the water slowly, accumulate it in our hands, use it almost immediately, and only a small unused quantity will be lost, unlike when the water is flowing strongly. If we wash our hands several times a day, when we do it for the first time, we can keep the water in a wash-

bowl, in which we can repeatedly wash our hands, or a bucket can be placed in the tub to accumulate the water used for hand washing. It could be written about how much water could be saved with a tool like this, however, we do not know how it works and who can re-use gray water. Anyway, when the sufficient quantity is accumulated, the toilet can be flushed with it. When tooth-brushing, we should also consider using the kind of toothpaste a portion of which will not flow down and drop into the sink. Apparently, this is not a big loss, but if half of the amount is lost each time, it is easy to calculate that we drain every second tube of toothpaste in the sink. The same applies to the use of shampoo or other cosmetics. We should consider getting cosmetics which, due to their consistency, can easily flow out of the tube or bottle, without leaving any residue, because if some of the material remains in them, it is nothing more than waste. Unfortunately, there are many products made even today, in which a part of the cosmetics contents remain, however, searching for solutions, Bharat Bhushan and Philip Brown[67], both American engineers, also started to work on the issue. Through their invention, they achieved that the contents flow out of flacons and bottles so as not to accumulate waste. Hopefully, this invention will soon be in production, and from that point it is worth paying attention to products which have these new characteristics, as only those should be bought.

Otherwise, we can also prepare toothpaste, several recipes can be found on some websites. Similarly, shampoo, soap, deodorant and deo can also be made, just as our great-grandmothers did. In the latter case, it is recommended to keep some of the purchased deo pumps or rollers and any other similar products, which can easily be refilled with our own make[68].

2. Although it feels good to sink in a large tub of water, but we should also think over how many showers it would be enough for, and

consider that Aniston can take a bath just in three minutes, so we can also succeed. Fortunately, not only the revered actress realized, but others too, including companies, that nowadays only bathroom devices can be produced that economize on water. A good example for this is OrbSys Shower[69], a shower utilizing space technology too, by the use of which 90 percent water and 80 percent energy savings can be achieved. The company estimates that EUR 1,000 can be saved per year by recycling the wastewater after having taken a shower, which can be used again. This is clearly not little money, but what somebody if does not have enough money to buy the products utilizing space technology? The easiest solution still remains. Having thoroughly moistened our body, it should be rinsed after an appropriate period of soaping.

As it was already written in the Preface, everyone should decide how far to go in changing their own habits and behavior. This is also applicable here, if we consider taking a bath in a tub. Although many may have aversions, it is still worth considering if it comes to taking a bath, whether or not another family member or more of them could take a bath in the same water. Actually, significant quantity of water can be saved by this method, so it is worth considering whether it could be applied, just like the two students' proposal. It is also worth mentioning here that the bathroom can be heated separately, and the family should bath in a row to take advantage of the currently generated heat. During the day, the bathroom should not be kept warm. Our biorhythms may differ, but we should harmonize them if possible.

It is also a question whether it is worthwhile to take a bath every day. Is it not enough to wash our intimate body parts and arm pits every other day? If we have a major wash basin or if we have bidet, these parts of the body can be easily washed. This question and similar ones should be answered individually. We heard it from the single and the young who work away that it regularly happens they do not even go out of the apartment for two days, and we heard some opinions that it is not worth wasting 40 liters of water for bathing, as average consumers do, because having a bath on a daily basis, including longer soaking in the tub, is otherwise not recommended by dermatologists. Their opinion is also supported by statistics, even if not entirely in this form, as statistical data[70] have shown since 2012 that the number of people who do not take a bath or a shower every day is increasing in American and West-European societies. In the UK, for example, almost half of the men and slightly less than one third of the women do not take a shower every day, and 12 percent of the population only take a thorough bath once a week. The reasons are complex, some fear for their skin for chlorinated water, which dries it, and there are people who want to protect the environment, and others do not find it natural. We just note for completeness that dermatologists find taking a daily shower essential, which, knowing Aniston's method, can be absolute saving as well, using much less water than having a bath in 40 liters of water.

Already in 2015, a press release published the case of a chemist, who claimed that he had not taken a shower or bath for 12 years, as he had learnt the method of animals, e.g. horses, cleansing themselves without water by watching them, and had developed a spray that blown onto the body would make bad body odor disappear. As a result of using his spray, David Whitlock[71] covers his skin with benevolent bacteria, which neutralize odors, and his invention was launched, known as Mother Dirt[72]. We have no knowledge about how successful the business has been, but we do know that we will never try the spray, and will rather stick to efficient washing.

Yet there is an exception: if we want to bathe in a tub and want to use 40 liters of water for that. Anyone can go to a swimming pool for relaxation purposes, which will serve their mental health.

3. You may want to reconstruct and provide your flat with water-saving taps, a toilet bowl, a bidet and a washing machine, and in the kitchen an eco-friendly dishwasher could be installed, if you are not using such appliances. They will certainly pay for themselves sometime, even if they are more expensive, it is the numbers that pay. Especially if the older devices are damaged and the tap starts dripping or there is a leakage of water. But not only this is the only aspect. A device is worth something if it works well and its use is optimal. For example, if it is difficult to set the right intensity of the water-jet the of the wash basin's tap, we may waste a lot of water to achieve the desired result. The same applies if it is difficult to adjust the water temperature before taking a shower, and we have to twist the tap here and there several times. It's no use having a perfect design if the device does not work properly. When purchasing, we should not only consider how attractive the device is, we should also take its water and energy efficiency into consideration[73]. During renovation or if we do not have one yet, a water meter should be installed in the appropriate part of the flat, by which it is easy to control the decreased quantity of water used and how much we have saved.

4. No toilet cleaning detergents existed 100 years ago, still our great-grandmothers not only could keep the toilet bowl clean, but the whole bathroom as well. They did not use anything else just vinegar and baking soda[74], which are still perfectly suited to the purpose, but many people buy much more expensive cleaning detergents, causing a significant additional cost to the household. Those who by all means want to scent their toilet, they might as well prepare their own toilet freshener[75].

5. It is also worth mentioning soap made by ourselves, as many use it. Not just one good recipe can be found on the Internet accompanied by video, so it is easy to learn how to make it. It is not uncommon to ask 2 or more dollars for an organic or natural soap at supermarkets, however, the same quantity can be made at a much lower cost if we make it at home, so much money can be saved[76]. All this is not only needed because of current economizing. If we settled in for self-sufficiency, we wash our hands far more times compared to the average, so this is one of the reasons we suggest to make our own hygienic supplies in larger quantities, so when there is a need, we just have to take it out and use it. It is not indifferent either how soap is stored during its use in the bathroom, i.e. the soap dish collects a lot of water and the bottom of the soap will be too humid, losing much of its value.

Soap is an excellent product, because it can be easily exchanged for something else or sold, especially among housewives. Homemade cosmetics are widespread and popular in many other countries today; moreover, there are places where not only its production is taught[77], but its marketing, product positioning and pricing, too. We can also make a living out of it, not so bad, the best example of which is deceased Burt Schavitz[78], who, in spite of living as a hippie, he became a millionaire thanks to his Burt's Bees product line.

Soap is used in a number of hotels, more precisely it would be fully used if the hotel guests took it away after one or two or several uses. Our habits, however, do not allow us to use hygienic supplies henceforward, so it goes into the trash. That is to say it would go there unless Clean the World[79], a non-profit organization had not started a particular program to collect redundant pieces of soap. The waste now promoted to be raw material is recycled by the non-profit organization, and then shipped to developing countries, the residents of which are unable to pay for basic toiletries either. In the course of its activities,

Clean the World has delivered 25 million bars of soap to 99 countries around the world, and this data illustrates in itself how squandering consumer society is in the developed part of the world, which comes in quite handy in countries, where there is a need for this. In developing countries, many people die at a very young age, in childhood, due to poor sanitation conditions.

Regarding soap, it is worth noting that in general we should pay attention to what the cosmetics available in supermarkets contain, and read the related product specifications. For example, if we want to buy a particular product, in this case anti-bacterial soap, it is worth considering what ingredients the item contains. According to the result[80] of a research published in a 2016 showed that antibacterial soaps in America are not better than conventional products, in fact, some of them may be harmful to health, so the substances named triclosan and triclocarban should be extracted from soap within a year, because if this does not happen, the product will be finally withdrawn from the market. Some manufacturers have started to comply with the official warning of the Federal Drug Administration (US Federal Drug Administration, FDA), however, according to the estimate of the Washington Post[81], there are 2,000 kinds of soaps still around in the US market, which contains at least one of these ingredients. This example shows how important it is to prepare our own cosmetics, in fact, own our food as well.

It is not only worth paying attention to how much better antibacterial soap can be compared to plain soap, but we should also consider in a particular case which product is more expensive or cheaper if we test whether liquid soap or block is cheaper. Many people consider liquid soaps more aesthetical and healthier, because they think that pathogens will colonize the surface of a bar of soap, so they do not use it, because they believe that liquid versions can only be more hygienic.

This assumption was refuted by an experiment organized by the New York Times[82/a], showing that even if there are bacteria on the surface of the soap, they will dissolve during use and removed together with the pathogen, which was already present on surface of the hand. Nevertheless, in recent decades, liquid soap has met with great commercial success, though handwashing can be even seven times more expensive[82/b] with it, compared to the use of bar soaps. From all this we can draw the conclusion, so if we see that compared to a conventional product a new product has appeared on the market, or hear that the new one is much more practical or better than the traditional one for some purposes, we should do a research to see how much more expensive it is. If the comparison shows that the old one still can be used, because it is basically capable of what it is expected to do, it may soon turn out that preferring the new version is just a waste of money. Not to mention that the plastic packaging liquid soaps will decompose in 400 years, and, of course, there is no need for that. Naturally, if we manufacture bar soap ourselves, not even waste paper will pollute the environment, which is formed after the purchase of soap at stores, and, in addition, our own products are cheaper than those bought at stores.

6. The water supply of our body is not a less important topic than economizing on water in the bathroom. Namely, on water, which is otherwise drinking water. As a matter of fact, in welfare societies, water arrives into households after filtering, although significantly chlorinated. Of course, man originally was not designed to drink chlorinated water, so for this reason, but also for other reasons, a variety of mineral waters have been introduced in the last few decades. This seriously charges our wallets, although we could drink cleaned tap water filtered at home, as we wrote about in the first chapter. It would be suitable just the same, but societies are quite divided in this respect. In 2013, for example, the distribution of bottled water was

banned in Concord, an American city[83]. Wells have been installed at various points in the town instead, where anyone could fill their bottles. The townspeople began to get used to the solution, so in 2014, when they had to vote on whether to keep the ban, 90 percent of the inhabitants voted against the distribution of bottled water in the city. If every town in the world applied a similar solution, it would cease the enormous environmental pollution caused by pet bottles, but this is hardly possible. As a result, consumers will continue buying mineral water, and so they will pay for it. If we consider that a person needs to drink approximately 3 liters of water every day, and 1.5 liter of average water costs a half dollar, anyone can calculate how much money is spent on daily, weekly and yearly consumption. Especially if we consider a family of four. That means a daily expense of 4 dollars, which will come to 28 dollars per week, and 1,460 dollars a year. A water filter used at home is of course much cheaper, it can be purchased for 20 dollars, however, filters have to be bought periodically for a few dollars and water charges have to be paid, but its application does not consume as much money as in the case water is bought at supermarkets. Indeed, if we get products from there, we always make the trader and the manufacturer richer, not ourselves. Of course, as it was written in the first chapter, we should get fresh spring water and store them in large capacity bottles if we can. This solution is the best of all, and it costs the least money.

7. The value of water is also shown in the World Bank's report in 2016[84], according to which water shortage will continue to be a direct cause for armed conflicts and migration. The most vulnerable regions are in Africa, the Middle-East, India, and China. One of the best-known war zones is in Syria, which has now almost completely destroyed the country. Experts claim that the other reason for all this was the drought[85] that occurred in 2006, which later led to warfare. The World Bank report also notes that 1.6 billion people on the

planet do not have enough water[86], and this figure will only increase in the coming years and decades. Presumably, in 2015, recognizing this problem led Bill Gates to advertise a machine that could produce potable and clean drinking water from faeces that is a kind of waste. According to the plan, the machine[87] will be deployed in areas where there are no established channel networks.

CARS AND MOTORING

In 2016, an American company, analyzing its own data, published a list of car brands, the maintenance of which required the most expense in the first 10 years of usage. The top five included three German car brands, the chart-topping BMW, Mercedes was the second, Audi was the fifth, while Cadillac and Volvo attained the third and fourth positions. From the sixth to tenth positions, however, only US cars appeared, and from there to Toyota, which occupied the 30th position, the field was changing. Although there is no big difference on the YourMechanic[88] list of the top ten, in respect of the average expenditure on car brands, a significant difference was detected between the first positioned BMW and the 22nd positioned Volkswagen, slightly more than double. However, if we look at the Google World Map[89] to check what car brands are searched for across continents, we will see that with Volkswagen much less interest is shown than in the service-intensive BMW. Although the search only reflects the interest and not the actual rate of purchase, it can be concluded that the majority of searchers do not really calculate the cost of operation, it is rather the brand that is in the center of interest. Of course, Google Maps was not created with the intent to show the service-intensity of cars or the evaluation of the YourMechanic statistics, still a sense of proportion can be perceived as to what basis serves for consumers to decide when searching for German car brands on the net. However, we ought to pay attention to the costs of operation, because it is not at all possible to save with a service-intensive car, and there could be huge differences between car models.

Today, however, not the operating cost and service-intensity of cars are the key issues at the dawn of the fourth Industrial Revolution, as the majority of car manufacturers are more concerned with the production of electric cars, as well as the introduction of driver or passenger controlled cars into transport. As described in the previous chapter, Ford[90] will take the lead in this market by 2021, that is within a few years, namely by manufacturing cars in which no gas, no brake, no steering wheel would be included. Of course, Tesla will also have to say something to these grandiose plans, or any other manufacturer, which is experimenting with the new technology. There is no doubt, however, that the ever more dynamic world of IoT highly encourages the spread of new types of vehicles, so the trend is clear, we will or have already stepped into the future, as according to Business Insider, there will be 10 million[91] driver or passenger controlled cars running around the roads by 2020, depending on the legal obstacles that may arise in the respective countries as opposed to the new technologies. Considering this, however, Tesla[92] has been working to develop fully automotive cars, and to create software for them. According to CEO Elon Musk, although he was criticized because of the safety of their cars, argued that completely automated cars would be safer[93] than man-guided vehicles. Elon Musk, however, does not do all this just to distribute cars, Tesla Networks[94] also wants to market a private transport service company, modelled on Uber, since it will not be a good business for him if car owners use his automated cars for providing Uber services, skimming off a fraction of the profit. The development, however, does not stop here. An 18-wheel truck of Otto[95], recently purchased by the Uber company, successfully delivered fifty thousand cans of beer from Fort Collins to Colorado Springs in October, 2016, travelling a hundred miles without a driver, who just oversaw the journey from the sleeper cab. This piece of news is not only interesting because it was the first successfully performed transport, but also because it clearly demonstrated that road truck traffic could be transitioned within a few years.

Similarly, news can be read about the penetration of electric cars, as there is no car manufacturer in the world that has not come forward with new models in the last couple of years. Their spread, however, could only be achieved through government subsidy so far, since they still have pretty stiff prices, and the distance that can be performed with a single charge is still short in many types of cars. Nevertheless, the direction of the development is already perceptible, as, for example, the Germans would not only ban gasoline-powered and diesel cars in their own country by 2030, but in the European Union also, creating harmful substance emission free urban and highway traffic conditions. With this measure, scattering the sky with rubbish would cease, at least it is certain in respect of transport, which would not only mean a serious step forward in climate change mitigation, but also in providing a cleaner urban air. According to the report[96] of WHO in 2016, the air is bad in 98 percent of large cities in underdeveloped and developing countries, while in developed countries it is steadily improving, but it is still significantly polluted in many cities, one of the causes of which

is obviously harmful substance emissions from transport. Bad city air resulting from vehicle emission is not only problematic because the air is intolerably stinky at the bustling parts of big cities, but also because, as stated in Nature Magazine[97], air pollution can cause the early death of 3.3 million people.

Until the distance performed on roads by electric cars with a single charge will increase, Plug-in hybrids can also be successfully sold[98]. Among big American car manufacturers, Chevrolet already has plans to roll out a new hybrid, perhaps in 2017. This car will be cheaper to maintain, since the auxiliary electric drive assists the combustion engine when required. In Europe, mainly in the VW group, BMW and Mercedes have developed this market in recent years, but of course other manufacturers have tried to catch up with them, such Toyota[99], producing hybrids

for the first time, which had calculated at least 300,000 hybrid car sales in the old continent, partly by introducing new brands as well.

Although car sales will grow in the world as a result of the self-driving or electric cars spread, and also due to the fact that more and more people can afford car purchase in the two most populous Asian countries, China and India, however, a further opposite trend can also be observed in America and the developed countries from the beginning of 2000s, as the rate of motoring has been reduced, most notably among the young and the elderly. The reasons may be different, according to a Washington Post blogger[100], multiple reasons can also contribute, involving young people too, among which the increasingly transforming labor market due to the digital revolution can also be mentioned, which allows teleworking. The teleworking young people have soon realized that there is simply no need for vehicles, or if there is, they can use public transport or car share[101], or possibly taxi services. In addition, young people began to undertake work in the city, if they could, choosing their place of residence within an easy reach providing easy approach in a short time, and preferably using urban public transport, riding bicycles, or just walk. Do young people travelling on a large city metro look familiar, browsing or playing on their smartphones? Yes, they are the ones who do not really have or need a car, because they cannot use the device while driving. Moreover, many young people are still repaying their student loans, so they simply cannot afford to buy a car and maintain it, nor can they ask for another loan, thus it also reinforces rejection vehicle purchase. In addition, the conditions of license acquisition have also become more rigorous in America, it is also more expensive to obtain, but motoring itself has started to become more expensive in recent years, discouraging young people from acquiring a driving license. It is not a negligible fact either that as a result of the global crisis, many young people have become unemployed, or not even able to get a job, so no car was needed. Just how IoT strengthens this process, it will become clear in a few years.

When autonomous or electric cars, or their combination have spread, it will also turn out what will become of present car parks. Especially if gas or diesel cars are banned in 2030 in respect to climate change, as planned in Europe, based on the German proposal. Presumably, the market will completely change by then, so conventional vehicles will already have been squeezed out, and even the cars bought today will have become worthless waste - this is the predicted scale of gaining ground of IoT within one and a half decades. Hopefully, some of their parts will be reused, and they will not provide such an ugly sight as the wreckages in the woods near a town called Chattilion[102], in Belgium.

Travelling by car is six times more expensive than riding a bike

In 2015, two universities, doing a joint research[103], analyzed whether motoring or cycle infrastructure should be developed in big cities, and concluded that travelling by car in cities was six times more expensive than riding bikes. The two institutions based their cost-benefit analysis on bike and car related social and individual expenses, namely on criteria such as accidents, climate change and air pollution, health, travel time or noise pollution. Although both cycling and motoring costs mean expense to society and state, still there was significant difference between the data. While the cost per vehicle was 0.50 cents/kilometer, in the case of cycling meant 0.08 cents, and the latter data could further be reduced if the development of cycle lanes encompassed the city. It does not have to be separately described that, besides society and the city, how much the person wins, who rides a bike wherever possible, as there is no need to pay for fuel, car repair service, and even the money that would otherwise be spent on car purchase can be saved. If we had a vehicle, but we sold it, we can do this comparison ourselves, but if we have never had one, we should compare the costs of a car owner, who leads the same lifestyle as we do. When we sold our car, we saved 5,000 dollars on fuel in a year, that obviously we have not even spent, and we also saved about 1,000 dollars on the servicing. Why did we sell it? There was simply no need for it, and actually not even before we bought it. As a matter of fact, we can get everywhere by car-sharing where we live, which does not consume more than a yearly average of 1,000 dollars.

With car or without?

If anyone wants to reduce transport costs associated with motoring, in the first round they should ask the question whether or not they need a car. Answering the question may be influenced by many factors, among which one of the most important is how workers can get to their workplaces. For example, in the Southern states of America and the wealthier Arab countries, almost everyone uses a car for this purpose, while in Northern Europe the bike is mostly used, mainly in big cities in Sweden, but also in Amsterdam and Copenhagen. In New York, every second employee uses the train and subways, and Tokyo can boast of almost the same good ratio, where two out of three people use public transport. In Switzerland, more precisely in Geneva, every third person walks to his or her workplace, and in Vietnam scooters and bikes present the vast majority on the roads[104]. Thus, so many countries, so many customs. So the question of whether or not to have a car is difficult to answer, and many people probably would say yes, even if they could do without a car, as people in welfare societies are accustomed to comfort, and it is difficult to give it up. Anyway, this question can be answered by anyone, if they do an experiment and avoid using a vehicle for a month or two. During this time it will turn out whether or not they can manage car-free transportation for a longer period. Of course, when we have sold our car, we will still have to pay, but the money spent on public transport or car-share will be much less than the amount paid for fuel. But even that can be saved if we ride a bicycle, just as the Scandinavians and Dutch people do.

Commuting to work or related car use can also be influenced by something else, namely, how much time workers devote to getting to work, typically to a spot in the city from within the city or from the outskirts, or even from the countryside. If this usually takes only half an hour, then it is considered to be ideal, as any worker, a cyclist in a given case would spend this time to getting to work. Over this time, many would choose their cars.

Other things may also have an effect on going to work by car. It is important how much time an employee has to go to work (a spot in the city) from a rural area or from a village. It is ideal if it takes only about thirty minutes, anyone can spend that much time with travelling or riding a bike. But if it takes more than half an hour, most people choose the car. Interesting calculations can be met[105] about how much time is spent commuting to our workplaces, and the figures are alarming. So why should we sit in a traffic jam if we can ride a bike, that can be a kind of sport, recreation and entertainment in one?

If anyone switches to biking, practically only the cost of the bike has to be paid, it is evident, however, that can occasionally be quite hefty, it could run up to hundreds of dollars. Of course, only if we buy a new one and we are not satisfied with a used bike, as the value of a newly bought bike will start decreasing almost immediately. Otherwise, just like in the case of cars, if we are lucky, we might as well buy the same 'coupled wheel' below cost, we just have to look around at what options are available on the market. Otherwise, when purchasing a bicycle, not only the price is the single aspect, we also have to consider what to use it for and where. If it is only used for urban travel, then obviously an ordinary bike will do fine, but for doing sports a different type is needed. It is worth browsing the net or asking an expert regarding such questions, because conscious shopping always starts with a survey, and it is worthwhile to review more specific, comprehensive detailed pages, webshops and Facebook groups to see the parameters of bikes on the market. In this regard, it is a must to make quality and price comparisons, otherwise we might lose a lot of money as well. There are traders who actually put together penny-worth bikes from unutilized parts, actually from waste, so if there is a service like this nearby us, it worth visiting, since in this case not only the waste will be recycled, but little money spent on a functioning bicycle.

As more and more people are buying bikes in the world, bicycles are getting better, they can be converted into electric bikes, if necessary. Of course, these hybrids have already been available on the market, still, in 2016, a company came up with an idea that is truly unique. If bikers cannot cycle the total distance, because they get tired or do not want to get sweaty completely on their way to work, the development called GeoOrbital[106] may come in handy, which produces the right speed using only the battery, and gets the cyclist to the destination. As it can be seen in the video[107] about the product, any bike can easily and quickly converted into an electrical bike using this tool, and the conversion can be solved in a few minutes. According to the manufacturer, even a 20-30 kilometer distance can be completed without a ride, which comes in handy for those who only use electric drive when going to work in the morning, and they no longer hurry on their way home, just ride, using their own power. The development enjoyed great success in 2016, despite its price was quite high, 649-699 dollars were asked for it when it was released, but even so many people buy it, because a bike with an included electric drive is still cheaper than a few-year-old used car. It is also cheaper than a scooter or a motorbike, and so they will become useless to buy, but of course the question is what means of transportation is suitable for the respective person.

Reliability tests

If we still buy a car, because it is essential for our work, it is worth studying the relevant reliability tests prior to purchase to see the car brands that are more effective for a longer term than others. Of course, there are so many tests and so many analyses, therefore many people prefer asking an experienced mechanic working at the site instead of dealers about the vehicles which have fewer problems than others, if they are considering a purchase. Nevertheless, some conclusions can be drawn from different tests, such as from the cited YourMechanic analysis, according to which not only the US, but also German cars are quite service-intensive, at least when we have a look at the top ten positions. The leader BMW requires an average of 17,800 dollars servicing charge, Pontiac in the eighth position 11,800 dollars, while Toyota in the twenty-fourth position only needs 5,500 dollars servicing charge over ten years. Warranty Direct, British insurance company arrived at similar results in 2015, though apparently used different methods than the US company, but similarly they took their own assessment for a basis. According to the list[108] made then, German cars do not perform very well, although only some types were listed among the least reliable brands. Of course, so many lists, so many results, therefore it is not surprising that Dekra[109], conducting technical examinations in Germany, which examined the reliability of cars that had performed 62,000 miles, listed several German cars among the first in different categories. Naturally, even more lists can be considered, but it is actually not the listing of individual car brands based on the surveys should be highlighted, but the fact that when purchasing a car, it should be at least as important to design the operation costs as the purchase price. Otherwise, a lot of money should be paid unnecessarily over the coming years. It is therefore advisable to choose a car with a better warranty, up to 5-7 years or 93,000 miles.

As it was written at the beginning of this chapter, we should plan ahead and choose our living space consciously, if possible, not only to achieve an energy efficient operation of the house, which should not be expensive. Moreover, the property should also have a garden to provide a possibility for partial self-sufficiency, as well as our workplace should be easy to approach form there, taking a short time at a cheap price, if we do not work where we live. The latter condition may be difficult to meet with a service-intensive car, so by all means we should change the car if the living space or the house is difficult to change for some reasons. Just think of what other things could be paid for over ten years instead of the service charges described by YourMechanic, for example, major expenditures could be repaid, mortgage credit where appropriate, however, many people still maintain their service-demanding cars, even if in fact there is no need for them. Egoism is boundless, one of the main characteristics of which is that many people travel alone in their vehicles, though they could share their cars with other commuters when going to work, without any major problems. The could share it with people who would contribute to the operation costs, saving a lot of money for the owner.

Of course, maybe in the future it will not present a problem where we live, we might as well be able to travel in self-driving air taxis with electric propulsion, as in 2016, Airbus[110] started working on it, with the intention of doing the first tests already one year later. The rush does not seem to be in vain, because there is a keen competition in this industry as well. The Chinese are slightly ahead, as tests have been carried out on their vehicle called Ehang184[111], even if just for only a short period of time, a bit more than 20 minutes, it is true, but it is already able to fly people in the air. Airbus would introduce a similar service like Uber, flying passenger without a pilot to the destination. According to the US company's project manager it will take about 10 years when air taxis are widely available in the world, revolutionizing urban transport, while eliminating traffic jams and standstills.

Will land transport really be replaced?

This question can also be put like this: Will the age of land transport, gas and diesel powered cars and therefore the age of oil-based societies gradually come to an end? Maybe, as besides Ford and Tesla's ideas, Airbus's example shows that the economy will gain more and more space for economy based on sharing in a couple of years, decades, while the future is simultaneously becoming the present.

However, technology can already help motoring society today, for example, if we want to organize our travel and transport in a cost-effective way, as Sygic navigation app[112] can communicate up-to-date information to us concerning where to find the cheapest gasoline, and where it is worth refueling. Users only need to provide the type and age of their car, and based on this data, the application will estimate the amount and cost of fuel, as well as it will show where gas stations are situated along the way. For example, if there is a gas station at half-way, which sells cheaper fuel, it is worth to refuel our car just enough to be able to get there, and continue refueling there, because this method also saves a lot of money. Especially in the case of gas-guzzling monsters. The app is not only interesting because its use can save money, save quite a lot where appropriate, but also because after a certain time, when the same distance is performed several times, for instance, it may involuntarily be etched in memory how much to assume in a complex way for the cost of gasoline or diesel within a period, such as a month. From here it is only one step to consider whether we need a car for every journey, or we might as well travel by train, which is usually much cheaper.

Anyway, today we do not even need to travel to the gas station if we do not want to, as a number of startups companies[113] have emerged and developed in the United States, which delivers fuel to homes. You do not need to do anything else, just click, and the service will come to your home. Although, refueling obviously will cost more than if you strived to travel to the gas station, but businesses still thrive, a number of them have thousands of customers on record. However, there is nothing extraordinary about it, the majority of car owners are not only egotistical, but also extremely convenient consumers. While business are spinning in America, Japan does not see the future in the establishment of mobile gas stations, but rather in the development of charging stations[114] for electric cars. By 2016, therefore, thanks to the government supporting the purchase of electric and hybrid vehicles, the country can already boast of 40,000 charging stations, as opposed to over 35,000 gas stations. The bulk of new charging stations are privately owned and are intended to satisfy the households' energy demand, the Japanese would reorganize the system according to the Airbnb model in the future, so anyone could have access to electric power, if there is an immediate demand for this.

The question of what could the future of public transport be, and in connection with this, whether there will be a demand for cars, yet is difficult to answer. There are some ideas that cars could be replaced with, such as Elon Musk's Hyperloop[115], besides the Airbus. As planned, the first Hyperloop track, mostly designed for carrying out tests, will be or would be built in the Nevada desert, and the next one between the United Arab Emirates and Dubai, which would already be a permanent line. It would be able to perform the 150-kilometer-long distance between Abu Dhabi and Dubai in 12 minutes[116], while the journey on the designed track of 600 km between Los Angeles and San Francisco would not take more than 30 minutes either[117] What's more, a fare in America would only cost 20 dollars, while currently the fastest and cheapest low-cost flight price is $ 60 at this distance, but even if the flight lasts only 70 minutes, you still have to add the travel time to and from the airport and the check-in time, which means three additional hours. Just to make sense of the difference, the same distance to the car costs $ 50 and the ride time is 6-7 hours. The facts are stubborn things, they say, the cheaper ticket and the lesser trip will decide what to do, but it's worth wondering if Hyperloop will be built and it will really work as Elon Musk promises.

An interesting solution was also presented by the Chinese to transform urban transport. As it can be seen in this video made about it, the idea is that TEB[118], i.e. Transit Elevated Bus would travel directly over car traffic, transporting up to 1,200 people from one station to another. The developers say that if the Chinese government approves the first investment, the first specific bus can be out on track in a year or so. If we watch the video[119] showing gigantic jams in China, it will immediately be clear why there is so much need for development.

The Chinese, however, would not only transform transport by establishing Elevated Transit Bus in the system. High-speed rail network is also under development at a phenomenal pace, Shanghaj Maglev already runs at a speed of 270 mi/hr into the city center from the Pudong International Airport, the goal, however, is to build a magnetic rail, which, surpassing the previous Japanese results, would keep a speed of over 370 mi/hr[120].

Of course, all these future developments will be most needed when traffic increases steadily in the world without a basic change in IoT work habits. Indeed, if a lot of people, or more precisely, more and more people can afford to work from home, as the Internet is already bringing the world into our homes, we will not have to go to work every day and so use public transport. This will turn out in a few years, yet we do not certainly have to be afraid that the world's public transport should not be developed, because in most countries of the world, especially in big cities, there is a serious problem.

Changing our habits

Significant savings can be achieved on fuel consumption by changing our own habits, as it is the numbers that pay. Certainly not everything can be written about, but who are urged to think by the presented examples, they may visit one of the websites dealing with this, where a lot of useful pieces of advice can be found. Have you thought about, for example, how much more energy a car consumes by unnecessary stoppings and starting, compared to going at slower speeds? We should try to avoid traffic jams in the city and use a well-functioning app, Waze[121] for instance, which shows the current position and where cars stop and go. In the same way, we should roll towards the traffic light if we expect it to turn green, and carefully observe the obstacles also, the bus stopping in front of us, the truck ready for loading, which is why we should also stop. If we are already stuck in a traffic jam, and there is stop and go in line, we should not follow the vehicle immediately in front of us if possible, as it may stop two or three times, when it is worth following. Why are these small changes important? Because starting requires 600 percent more fuel consumption, compared to traveling at a slower speed.

When we start out somewhere, we should do it in adequate time to have the necessary time to get to our destination when expected. To our workplace in the morning or to a business meeting. Whoever is behind schedule, not only press the accelerator harder, but, no matter how strange it may sound, the brakes too. Just think of when you expect the light to switch to red, but still you want to reach it to get through and to be able to turn right, what speed we should approach the light and the push the brake when arriving there and start turning right. When the speed limit is exceeded, a fine can be expected, and this is to be avoided, but it is not going to be highlighted now in this example. There are many drivers who travel at high speed toward the lights, even when not in a rush, more exactly they push the gas pedal until they get to the light, and then firmly push then brake and take a curve. Such ill-practiced techniques should be avoided, as we lose much more energy by pushing the brake and then giving full throttle, than traveling at a normal speed.

If we switch to more economical driving, the end result may be that either registered in an app or counted in mind, we will see how much fuel we have saved each month, thanks to new methods. The total savings can also be calculated, so we should not be surprised if the difference may be up to hundreds of dollars a year.

Car washing

An average car wash may consume even 150-200 liters of water, so it is not an environmentally friendly solution. When in 2015, there was a severe drought in California, a Volvo manager in San Diego started a campaign in order to reduce water consumption. Driving Dirty[122] caused a general consternation in people, and at the same time the action proved to be quite awareness-raising. Car owners were requested not to wash their cars for at least one month to save 18 million gallons of water, and then they could take photos of the results, upload and share them on community sites, so anybody could see the results of the campaign, also inciting others to economize on water.

Of course, really environmentally friendly solutions are also known today so as not to waste 53 gallons of water on cleaning cars per car wash. According to a company's video[123], dirt can be removed from the car by dry washing, without water usage. The detergent also known as car shampoo works simply. When applied to the surface, it creates a protective film on particles that would scratch the cars, so the body of the car can easily be cleaned. In addition, the specific product is absolutely environmentally friendly, it is not harmful to plants or any other organisms. If anyone checks up on the Internet how much a product lacking water use costs and how many washings it is enough for, and also calculates how much is spent on car cleaning at car wash or even at home, it can be decided which product or service should be used. Of course, for this, we should also know how much water is consumed with washing each time.

Naturally, no cleaning has to be financed if we do not own a car. In this case, no dirty water is produced, nor do we have to spend on shampoo, and it is the best waste, which is not created.

Smart cities, the relation system between motoring and cycling

No longer of the future, but the city of the present is being built in Vienna[124], a city with a smart green technology that offers a more economical way of life to its residents. From the outset, it was designed for this purpose, but the Aspern Smart City Project is interesting for other reasons as well. The operators of the already constructed buildings continuously collect data resulting from the residents' energy use. They are even interested to know what happens to the energy or heat produced by the engine of the car parked in the garage. It is not a coincidence that they do so, as it only turns out in practice how the electric power use and the energy consumed for heating and cooling can be optimized, therefore the project is actually a scientific experiment, capable of self-development, based on which more and more suitable buildings can be constructed in Aspern in the coming months and years. Buildings that do not waste energy, and thus they do not produce waste. Although the data and feedback only cover one year, since the first residents moved into the first buildings a year ago, the development enjoys great success, tenants like to live there and life is not just better, but cheaper too.

Aspern not only aims for an optimization of energy use, but that of transport as well. It is based on solutions that would hinder traditional use of cars, more precisely, their being unused. For this purpose, community driving would be introduced, as according to the designers, the emergence of autonomous cars will not otherwise require one or more cars per family, and people will opt for community automotive transport. Not least because this solution will obviously be much cheaper than purchasing and maintaining a car, which, according to the statistics, in 90 percent of the day is otherwise unused in a parking lot somewhere. Within a few years, it will turn out whether the idea works, which may also be influenced by the time needed to perform the same distance by car and using public transport. According to the data, it takes half an hour to get to the city center by metro or train, and by car the same distance can be performed in one hour, even if the route is not busy or jam-packed. Aspern also attaches great importance to bicycle traffic, so cars are banned from the main roads, and only bikes are allowed in the smart city, thereby promoting the idea that the Viennese should not use cars, rather they should buy and ride bikes.

PROVISIONING

The purchase of the house or apartment

Purchasing a property should not only be planned in terms of energy consumption or transportation, as it was mentioned in the first chapter. In our changing world, on the threshold of the fourth industrial revolution, it is worth buying a house, if we have not already done so, which has several advantages, including a garden, and thus allows the production of a part of our own food supply. If we live in a city apartment and do not have a garden, we still have the opportunity to purchase the food directly. We will discuss this topic later, but for now we should remain at house purchase.

Before going into detail, you might want to read a few words about employment, one of the main organizing principles of our lives, as you may have read about it previously. In accordance with the 20th century way of life, the employees moved to large cities or they were already born there, and when they finished school, they undertook a job in the hope of assuring their livelihoods. This trend, however, seems to disintegrate, the ever expanding world of IoT it is not or is hardly required to commute to work, as a diversity of work will be done from home in a few years or within the decade. In fact, many kinds of work can already be done or could be done from home, however, companies have not yet begun to incorporate complete developments, by which they would completely be transformed, and thus their office jobs, factory jobs and other workplaces would become superfluous. As long as lockouts will not occur in some sectors, people tend to ignore this negative tendency and neglect it. However, they should care about it, as the trend shows that workers should consider the near future and possible versions, and learn more than one trade, adapting to the new system, lest one day to the next an existential crash would occur in their lives. For example, a crash that involved several American families after the economic crisis in 2008.

We should give an example here, our own case[125]. I work as a defense attorney, and my partner is a bank clerk. About a decade ago, I realized that due to technical progress, the attorney's office became almost entirely unused, as I met one client no more than once there, but not afterwards, when the cases had to be managed at the police station when applicable or at the court, if the case continued there. We were able to talk what we had to by phone or exchange information by e-mail, so for this reason the client did not even have to come to my office. In 1993, when I started my career, I obviously worked with an assistant and an attorney candidate, regularly commuting to my office. From 1996 to 2000, however, there was less and less work for my assistant, so she had to resign, because she was simply replaced by the mobile phone and computer, as a result digitalization and gaining ground of the mobile phone. From then on, even I have had to go to my office fewer and fewer times, and today there is hardly any need to do so. Data is stored in flash memory sticks or other data media instead of files, and I take my notebook to the court instead of a briefcase. It would already be possible, of course, not to go to the court building for proceedings, as we could also be present at the hearings, using Skype, however, this has not yet been applied. Practically, I hardly see the postman, he used to come day by day, delivering literally bulks of letters, now all received in e-mail. As computer programs are getting better, and better performing algorithm and robots come to light, I had to think over whether I as an attorney could be replaced by a machine, and if so, when. This question is still quite difficult to answer relying on my present knowledge, but probably yes, in addition, in a short period of time, as short as few years, because it is nothing more than a simple programming issue. In 2015, TomorrowToday Global[126], American futurist organization, took almost the same view, according to which people having similar occupations to attorneys, such as accountants or statisticians are at risk, as well as lawyers themselves. However, in the organization's view, not only they, but also professionals working in the financial markets may go packing, such as financial advisors and stock brokers, as well as bankers. All this means that my partner and I may be left without a job within a decade, robots will replace us.

However odd it may sound, hearing this piece of news, it did not make us feel desperate. A few years ago, there was information available showing that we should change and adapt, even if not to the world created by IoT. One piece of information showed that food prices would continuously raise year by year, from decade to decade, which would be true of energy related expenses, so those who could afford should start producing their own food or energy to be consumed, as the old world seemed to crumble and become unsustainable. The fact that we recognized why adaptation, i.e. the transformation of our lives was so much in focus, was actually the result of chance, not only due to conscious thought. A few years ago, when browsing some new publications in a bookstore, Tim Harford's book entitled Adapt[127] found its way to our hands. Besides being a very interesting and readable work, it also has an important message to the readers. According to this, we must exercise continuous control over our own life, no matter how sable or static it seems, because a change may occur any time, just like the 2008 financial crisis, which, if we do not adapt properly or we are not sufficiently far-sighted, we may lose all we have. Of course, we may argue about how the 2008 financial crisis could be seen by average people, and whether we could have prepared for that, but that's the very moment when that needs to make us think and urge us to make the appropriate steps. Our world is never static, it never provides constant security, so if possible, we should learn more than one trade, even when apparently there is no need for that, or only just read news articles on food and energy prices being continuously raised, having little news value for average people. When in 2015 we read the first pieces of news about what changes the fourth industrial revolution could bring into our lives, we finally decided to move to the countryside as soon as we could, partly giving up our former city life, and start a self-sufficient life, as much as possible. It will turn out in a few years or a decade what the world of IoT brings, but in the meantime we will continue to work if we can, because so far, fortunately we have had work to do, still besides this, we will also form our self-sufficiency.

PURCHASE PRICE AND RESERVE

In general it can be said that rural properties are much cheaper than those which we can be bought in cities, although differences still arise. Let's look at our example. Our 960-square-feet house[128] has a plot of 5580 ft² , which was approx. half as expensive as a similar detached house in the city if we had wanted to buy one, and it also proved to be cheaper compared to the apartments there, having the same size of ground-space. Why is it worth emphasizing this? If you change from the city to the countryside, as we did, and sell your property in the city, typically an apartment, you can purchase a house and start your own food production if you have a little money left over and form a reserve. Money reserve is especially important, it is almost certain that you will need it in the future, and it will come in handy if you are not successful at the beginning in terms of self-sufficiency, and therefore food supplies should be provided from other sources. Thus, the surplus due to the fact that we purchased a house in rural area at a cheaper price was only apparent, as a part of it was spent on restauration, as well as on food we lacked.

THE PURCHASE PRICE IN ITSELF IS NEVER A DECISIVE FACTOR

Not only the purchase price, but other aspects had to also be taken into account when we decided to buy the chosen house. Beyond question, among the considerations the operation of the house in and energetic sense proved to be one of the most important factors. Luckily, we managed to find a house, the costs of which amounted to much less than other properties in the area, as it could be noticed, thanks to the masterly insulation of the building and other parameters, and to the fact that had been previously restored. What did that mean in numbers? In summer, when the outside temperature was 95-104 °F, the thermometer did not rise above 77 °F inside, so the air conditioning did not have to be used, not even if it was installed. We had hybrid heating, it could also be solved with wood, which proved to be much cheaper than if you just heated with natural gas.

Another important aspect was not to spend too much on transport, as it also has to be considered if you buy a house. Since we live close to the city, 30 minutes from it, we commuted using public transport or car-share services back and forth. The bus tickets occasionally amounted to one dollar, so we did not need a car thereafter and sold it. However, we did not want to move farther away, because our relatives and friends continued to live in the city, so we did not wish to waste more time than 30 minutes travelling when visiting them, since unnecessary rides are nothing else but waste. For longer journeys we used the railways, coach or car-share services, despite the fact that they may not actually be as convenient as using an own car. However, if discomfort was caused during the trips, we always remembered the fact that we did not have to pay anything for car maintenance or fuel, which should not be underestimated, except of course when sharing a car. As described previously, we used to spend a yearly average of 5,000 dollars only on fuel, 1,000 dollars on car service, making it easy to calculate the amount of money that has enriched the family budget since then. However, there are some aspects other than property operation costs, which cannot be or are difficult to financially measure.

The neighborhood of the house is quiet, a huge forest, a protected landscape area lies in the immediate vicinity, with a lot of animals in our natural environment. It is absolutely suited to an exhausted person to retract from the noise of the city and rest, and when mentally refreshed, to go back to work.

Of course, the benefits or the aspects to be considered when purchasing a house could be further listed, but so far quite enough has been discussed to show what other criteria may be taken into account when we buy a house, besides the price of the house.

The result

A few months after moving in, we started to realize that we were able to achieve significant savings, as a result of economizing and settling in for a partly self-sufficient way of life, and, at the same time, two years later, we could also survive the crisis, which shook the entire world in 2008. This means that we are able to adapt.

The size of the garden

Opinions differ on how big the garden of a house should be if we wish to settle in for self-sufficiency. Theoretically, there is no clear answer to the question, however, there are some gardeners who, through professional knowledge are able to grow more than two tons of vegetables and fruits, as well as cultivate spices and herbs in 478 yd^2, just as the Desarves family of four members does in Pasadena[128]. Otherwise, a professional, who has long been engaged in local gardening, quickly provides information on what and how or how much to grow, as in lack of it, we cannot even carry out an estimate if we are absolute beginners, we would not know the approximate quantity that can be achieved, or what we actually need. To all this, however, should also be added that if you do not succeed in growing some vegetables or fruits for the first time, you should not panic, as gardening will absolute live up to your expectations after a while.

What about townspeople?

Not even those living in a city should despair who only have a small garden, because the developments in technology allow smarter and smarter tools for growing vegetables even in the backyard. According to Californian company called FarmBot Inc. [129], only a five-foot-wide land is needed to deploy the FarmBot device, launched in 2016, growing the most basic vegetables for us. The video about the robot shows that the machine performs all the work instead of us, such as planting, watering, removing weeds, and only harvesting is left for us. Meanwhile, the robot applies the best technology, it implements well-designed crop combinations, it utilizes solar power and even rainwater, but it does not produce waste or use chemicals. In addition, it is also provided with an open source code, i.e. anyone can easily build one at home, at least it is promised by the developers. Whether the robot will be widely applied, it will turn out in the coming years, but city-dwellers still have the well-established options of community agriculture or the operation of urban gardens until then.

As is known, community or community-supported agriculture[130] started gaining ground a few decades ago and by now it has spread throughout the world. Although CSA communities may be very different, they essentially agree to form a kind of community awareness. In this community, there is a direct contact between farmers and members, the latter financing the prices of crops and the costs of operation in advance. In this system, the members receive the vegetables and fruit, or animal products at specified intervals, but also share the risks, for instance, if a kind of fruit or vegetable crop fails. The advantage of these kinds of agriculture compared to large-scale farming and supermarket chains sales is undoubtedly that these communities do not have to pay trade benefits, i.e. purchase at stores is not charged by compulsory profit. This makes farms generally not using chemicals competitive in the food market, as opposed to poor quality dumping goods from the outset, so the participating community members will gain absolutely healthy food in proportion to price value, unlike at supermarkets, even if, of course, at a bit more expensive price. Therefore, this is the main reason why it is worthwhile and rewarding to become a community member, which can otherwise be formulated in a way that the members of the community operating a sustainable and absolute eco-system lacking waste production, they are able save a lot of money, because if they had to buy the same goods at supermarkets marketing organic foods, they would obviously have to pay more. The advantage, however, not only manifests itself in saving money, but the members constitute integral parts of the community, they can visit the farm even on a regular basis, they can have their children taught agriculture and stock-farming, i.e. an alternative lifestyle, where real human relationships can be built and true friends can be gained, while they can have healthy food in a modern way and pre-plan their diet in order to remain healthy. Such people do not or rarely need to attend expensive medical treatments, and they spend little or do not spend on medicines at all.

Besides agricultural community, city dwellers lacking a backyard have another option to grow their vegetables and fruits that is a city garden. It may happen that there are quite serious communities on major social networking sites, such as Grow Food, Not Lawns[131]. They have more than 800,000 followers on their Facebook page, as well as great articles that can be read on urban gardens, the applicable technologies there, such as on Will Allen, on community sites operated by websites, however, this site is not only interesting for this reason. Even the choice of name is very expressive and suggestive to call attention that if city dwellers possess a garden, a vegetable garden should be operated in it, instead of growing a lawn.

There are historical examples that inevitably gave rise to urban gardens. To ensure that Cubans do not die of famine, they were forced to dispossess all green areas in major cities, which could be transformed into gardens[132]. All this occurred when the Soviet Union collapsed and was no longer able to feed the island country through umbilical cord, which naturally was forced to import oil. Owing to the absence of fuel, large-scale agriculture collapsed within a few days, so the Cubans were forced to look for alternatives, creating urban gardens, one after the other. Cuba has reached a self-sufficient condition today in terms of organic fruit and vegetable production, however, meat can barely be produced, since meat production, more specifically fodder production requires large quantities of oil. Despite this, however, many Cubans are in perfect health as a result, they hardly suffer from diseases of civilization due to the diet largely based or fruits and vegetables.

In connection with the above, it is worth highlighting an important point. Those who in one way or another deal with self-sufficiency, they call a system into life that is always able to renew and will remain operational even if another crisis comes. Some analysts predict that serious food supply problems may occur in welfare societies by 2030, as our arable lands are going to be exhausted. It is not difficult to imagine what will follow as a result, not just big stores will be left out of supply, but consumers also.

Among our resources, not only oil or water is running out dramatically, but soil as well. The total land area is 149 million square kilometers, out of which 20 million km² is cultivated area, and 7.1 million km² of arable land. 0.3 hectares of cultivated land and 0.1 hectares of arable land come to the currently 6.8 billion people living on Earth, which is very little. In addition, 75 billion tons of soil is eroded every year[133]. The data properly illustrate just how food production of humanity is becoming unsustainable, but man does not change anything, although fundamental changes would be required. Many people see the solution in the transition to community agriculture.

We will see what the future brings, and whether there will be a need to massively organize our self-sufficiency at the earliest in 2030, as the Cubans did, when the Soviet Union collapsed.

Knowledge

Interesting ideas sparked the program development of a seemingly simple, yet ingenious-minded American teacher[134], who begins his captivating video presentation like this: 'Good afternoon. I am not a farmer. No. But I am a parent, and I live here, and I am a teacher. This is my world.' I wonder why the teacher living in Bronx started his speech like this. The answer is very simple. Stephen Ritz stared to realized that as a result of outdated malnutrition his students were getting fatter and sicker, and tried to help the problem by creating a school horticulture for them, although, in fact, he did not know much about growing plants. He did a lot more afterwards, he did not only teach his students to grow plants and healthy nutrition, but how to change and improve their lives, too. Most of the students in fact were disadvantaged, many of them were homeless or lived with their foster parents, but when they realized how to earn money and create a livelihood by crop production, through the example they understood that it was not impossible for them to break out of poverty and isolation, i.e. to continue their studies and become successful.

A similar program was founded by the new dean[135] at Paul Quinn College in Dallas, who had the football field cracked and ploughed, creating a vegetable garden, after having noticed that the team had lost their matches, one after the other. With this symbolic step, Michael Sorrel made it possible for students living in disadvantaged circumstances to earn money by working in the garden so as to establish their financial conditions and pay their annual tuition fees. The story is interesting not only for this reason, but also because of what the program provides. Accordingly, by gaining proper experience, the students learned to write business plans, how to handle revenues and expenditures in a planned way, i.e. to establish a long-term strategy. They acquired knowledge that later could be used in other areas, for example, if the students would want to start their own businesses. 'Where others see hopelessness, we can see an opportunity' - one of the students, Vincent Owoseni, conveyed his opinion through a PBS report on a US public television[136]. All this sums up well what organic gardening and education for self-sufficiency are capable of, as well as the proper knowledge of a dean.

The incomes of the few Brooklyn young guys do not originate from cultivation, but kitchen waste collection, as they regularly visit the cooperating local households, transporting organic waste remaining at households after the preparation and consumption of meals by bicycle and transforming it into compost. By creating BK Rot, a compost community[137], the goal of Sandy Nurse and Renee Peperone was not only

to organize recycling of waste and thereby setting up a model that could also be used elsewhere, but also to show an example and vision for young people in an area, where actually one could hardly find work, and the rate of crime was very high.

Just as Stephen Ritz, Jamie Oliver also gave an ever since very successful presentation[138] on TED, viewed by millions, drawing the attention as to why we needed to teach our children to cook, i.e. even if we did not teach them farming, at least they should learn self-catering. The reason is simple. As a result of fast-food menus, food bought in supermarkets and sweetened foods many adults die prematurely in America or in the United Kingdom, however, when properly nourished in a healthy way, at least they would live to retirement age. According to the world-famous chef, however, there is more to this problem than that. Adults not only eat themselves to death, but, unfortunately, they provide the same foods to their children as well, causing diseases or death to many. What would the solution be? They should simply be taught how to prepare healthy meals, either at school or at home.

While obviously Jamie Oliver did or could not talk about this fact, still it is clear that the introduction of unhealthy food into human organism and its relation to obesity is virtually nothing more than excess fat, i.e. production of waste in the organism. In addition, medicine considers obesity a disease in itself[139], and, at the same time a condition, that can be the basis of a more serious disease of civilization and related formation of death. Unfortunately, ordinary consumers know almost nothing or very little about the fact that obesity is a disease in itself, and in the absence of symptoms they believe that they are healthy. And when faced with the fact of how improperly nourished, in many cases, a disease has already formed that can even cause death. According to a recently published research[140], the list of death causing factors in welfare societies is led by malnutrition, followed by smoking and obesity. In America, one of five people dies of this strange disease too soon, while in Europe every seventh.

It is thought-provoking that some consumers still spend a lot of money to get sick or even die, while once again spend a lot of money on medical treatments and medicines to get healed, but obviously all this is done so because they do not have proper knowledge, there is no better word for it, to 'ab ovo' serve their survival.

It is useful to have healthy food, and compile a daily or weekly diet for this purpose, and cook for ourselves and thus stay healthy, as suggested by Jamie Oliver.

Food production and drawing up nutrition and dietary plans

160

We had our own experiences related to the initial difficulties of food production described above. During the first year we had to invest 300 dollars in gardening tools, water pumps, seeds and seedlings to be able to start our own organic vegetable and fruit production. What we produced only accounted for 150 dollars, this would have been the cost of buying these products at the organic market, this means that our investment did not result in any tangible profit. This also means that in case if we only relied on this type of food production or food supply, both of us would have died of starvation during the summer. The cause of this was, by the way, that we started gardening quite late, we bought the real estate in May and the local savvy who could have helped us with his knowledge about organic farming and food production as for which vegetables grow together best locally was too busy at the time to come and survey what sort of vegetables we should plant and in what sort of combination. As a result, some plants, such as cucumbers were almost entirely devastated by plant diseases – although we tried to prevent it – in spite of the fact that harvest was quite good at the beginning; tomatoes were also decimated. However, there were some vegetables, such as eggplants, or fruits, for example inherited grapes which brought really great harvest, fighting plant diseases. In spite of all this, we can state and draw the conclusion that in the absence of appropriate knowledge we lost lots of potential harvest and besides the active we produced a significant amount of passive harvest, that is, waste, for which we are to be blamed. Next year we will calculate our budget so that we spend 10-20 dollars for seeds and seedlings, 300 dollars for fertilization and we will produce organic vegetables and fruits in the value of 500-700 dollars. The reason for this is that we do not need more, therefore we try to make the calculation in such a way that we do not produce a significant amount of surplus, if yes, we can swap them for fruits, eggs, goat's milk or any other food that we do not produce and which is available locally, otherwise we don't do anything else but produce waste.

This example demonstrates that despite the difficulties growing your own food has a great significance nowadays. This is the food ingredient that is exempt from all kinds of chemicals, cannot be GMO, of course, and regarding its vitamin and fiber content it is of much better quality than the vegetables and fruits available in supermarkets. If we produce food at home, we can save a lot of costs since we do not have to add the profit of retailers and wholesale producers but the advantages shall not only be translated to financial terms. People who grow their own food which is produced in modern, sustainable and healthy ways will not become sick, unlike those who buy food in supermarkets, especially processed food. The vast majority of these processed foods have not even existed 100 years ago.

Eating modern and healthy food and obtaining food ingredients which we cannot produce ourselves, that is, drawing up our diet can be as complex as gardening itself. However, it is worth the effort since we can save a lot of money and we shall not be our own enemy. How can we decrease the money needed for buying food and to eat well and lead a healthy life at the same time? The case of the English mother of three[141] is a good example for this, she turned her back on buying things at the supermarket and she started to order food ingredients online in great quantities, including of course vegetables and fruit, obviously a lot cheaper. Kate Haigh spent 130 pounds in supermarkets on a weekly basis and by switching to purchasing food online, in great quantities – not contributing to supermarkets' profit – she reduced this amount to 60 pounds. Since she decided to prepare their own food, she always had to cook but in her opinion she got used to it quickly and she managed to produce a variety of healthy dishes from the same food ingredients, since there are lots of suitable recipes available on the internet. Her objective was not only to cook much cheaper and better quality dishes but also to avoid waste production during cooking, since she considers that wasting food is a form of greed. Therefore she only cooked as much as her family could eat, if there were any leftovers, she used it for tomorrow's dishes again. As the press reported, the smart housewife uses lots of vegetables and fruits for her dishes and she only orders high quality meat in great quantities. She freezes it in portions and uses the portions one by one. Since the family owns a small garden, next year they plan to produce some vegetables themselves, thus they would like to cut down on the 60 pound shopping costs even further.

As if we were reading our own thoughts, but if we consider it really, there is nothing special in trying to cut down on costs and trying to eat healthy and modern food at the same time. Moreover, doing it in such a way that one does not produce any food waste, this is the mentality everyone shall adopt. Everyone can compare this way of thinking to their own and considering how much food lands in the garbage on a monthly basis, we can immediately see how much we waste superfluously.

In 2013, the program[142] was launched in America for waste food reduction, since wasting has increased from the '70s onwards, e.g. almost half, actually 40 percent of the food produced was transported to landfills in 2013. In a daily breakdown it meant that a US citizen threw an average of 1,400 calories worth of food out into the trash each day, which resulted in wasting $ 400/person/year. The data are striking, but unfortunately welfare societies will continue to waste, so it is no wonder many people are 'forced' to go on a diet on a yearly basis.

We have never tried fashionable diets and not because the one that is successful should not be useful, but because the best way 'to lose weight' is not to lose anything, following the principle that the best waste is the waste that has not even be produced. Decades ago this idea was formulated by John Yudkin[143], the author of several books as follows: 'There are no secrets to regulating our body weight. Those who eat more calories than the calories needed for the operation of their bodies are putting on weight. Those who eat the same amount as required will retain their figure. Those who eat less will lose weight. I know it from experience that people find it hard to accept this simple fact.' [144]

However, if we start organizing our own food supply, including our dietary habits, reducing waste production to zero, after a while we will be able to calculate precisely how much caloric value intake we need on a daily basis, thus keeping our body weight and health. After a certain amount of time this goes on by itself, by calculating calories in our minds, we can find lots of tables including the calories content of food per 100 grams and cooking based on our calculations. If it does not go smoothly, we can consult doctors and dietitians for expert advice, moreover, it is recommended, and there are some applications, such as Incentive[145] which may further help these processes. Incentive and other similar apps award you each time you reach a certain goal, regardless of their significance, thus they encourage you to go on. By calculating calories on a daily basis, many people managed to lose weight in the world, the media keeps reporting about such cases. Recently, about a 29 year old mother of two, living in Kentucky. After some unsuccessful attempts, two years ago Amy Leroy[146] started another diet during which she downloaded an application designed for counting calories. Based on the table, she calculated that she eats 4000 calories a day, thus when she reduced it to the appropriate level, she started losing weight. If we look at the photos of Amy taken earlier and now, we can hardly recognize her. She used to weigh 158 kg and now she weighs 68. As if we were looking at another woman: in the new photos Amy is pretty and sporty. According to the mother, this is not the only success, she also regained her health and today she is happy to live a healthy life again.

The Smart Belt[147] was designed especially for people wishing to lose weight. After the sufficient money was collected on Kickstarter for starting the business in 2016, this tool has been useful for people wishing to lose weight. During its operation the Smart Belt sends information to our smart phone how much we have eaten, how much time we spent sitting during the day at our workplace, how many steps we have made, thus calculating the calories[148] that we have to lose and whether we have to change our dietary habits and lifestyle. It is not only recommended for those who are prone to overeating but also for those who would simply like to see weekly or monthly data.

After a while, regardless of whether we use some apps or not, there will be certain menus in our diet, sometimes they might need to be updated, for which the internet or Pinterest can be useful.

However, before starting any diets, it is worth asking the doctor's or the dietitian's advice to set the appropriate amount of calories, whether it can bring the appropriate results. It might happen that the appropriate results cannot be achieved, in these cases another treatment is required, but also in cases when besides reducing the amount of food other methods can also be applied.

Buying food and dietary habits

Those who partly rely on self-sufficiency cannot avoid going to the supermarket and buying some products there. Products, such as bananas, coffee or rice, that cannot be produced locally, can only be bought in supermarkets. These are the occasions when one is tempted to buy other things, too, which one would not buy otherwise. During these visits to the supermarkets one tends to behave like a normal consumer who goes to the supermarket without a specific plan or shopping list, therefore if we can, we should define exactly what we would like to buy and we should not diverge from the list. If we buy additional things as well, we will also diverge from our dietary plan and after a while we will live as an average consumer. All this does not mean of course that we have to live as puritans and we are not allowed to buy other things from time to time but we have to find the middle ground otherwise our health will suffer. While reading these lines you can think you would not be tempted, but supermarkets – as we mentioned before – apply such methods certified by scientific observations and psychological tests, supported by studies[149] that you can easily find yourself thinking about buying this or that cheap product. Discounts, buy one get one free, while stocks last and other marketing solutions may easily manipulate you, making you spend more and more money in supermarkets. Even if we go to the supermarket equipped with a list, at least according to an Australian survey. The survey ordered by the LiveLighter[150] foundation revealed that although two-thirds of the average Australian consumers were keen on healthy eating and they planned their weekly diet, moreover, they did not only calculate with caloric values but compared prices, too, despite this they were prone to temptation. Out of three interviewees three admitted that besides healthy food they also succumbed to buying some products considered unhealthy, mostly chocolate, soft drinks with high sugar content, ice-cream, and chips. The reason for this was that these products were installed near the path leading towards the counters, encouraging the so-called impulse customers to neglect the basic principle of conscious buying practices to also buy unhealthy products which they originally did not intend to buy. Little costs can accumulate, thus the average consumer will pour lots of money down the drain during one month or one year, according to the data, 53% of Australians goes to supermarkets several times weekly, many of them go there even on a daily basis. This money contributes to the income of supermarkets, significantly profiting from even impulse buyers. There are some data certifying the successful sales technology of supermarkets: 35% of an Australian's energy intake is derived from unhealthy food which contributes to 63% of adults and 27% of children being overweight. Being overweight can be the ground for many illnesses whose treatment or the later diets can cost lots of money, too.

In spite of all these things the average consumer doesn't do anything else but consume and consume, that is, keep wasting money and resources. They buy food and process it by cooking in such a way that they throw away parts of it, producing waste. Of course not every day but in many cases but this is enough for one-third of the food ending up in garbage bins[151]. This is a huge number in itself but it also means a great cost on the level of the consumer as well, in spite of all this many people do not mind it, only if it can be translated into terms of money how much they wasted for unused products on a weekly or monthly basis. This solution was applied by the producers of the successful Wa$ted![152] TV series in 2008 when they filmed the lavish lifestyle of average consumers. The participants of the reality show undertook to lead a more economical life during a period of 3 weeks, that is, they wouldn't be wasting a part of the food they bought. At the end of the 3 week long period they received the amount from the moderator as a reward for their achievement, a sum of money that they would have spared, had they led a more conscious life. This proved to be very efficient, made many people think and the reality show gained international fame.

The action of the environmental campaigner, Rob Greenfield[153] also proved to be very efficient in 2016; he stacked a smaller pile of garbage on himself, touring the streets of New York during 30 days, demonstrating the daily and monthly amount of waste accumulated by an average consumer. Since an American produces about 2 kg of waste each day on average, on the last day the bizarre looking campaigner walked around the city with 60 kg on him. His action was reported not only by the American journals, magazines and the international press but there will also be a film on his action. As long as the film is not presented, Rob's program and philosophy is broadcast through his TV channel, providing lots of information how you can learn a lot about how you can reduce the waste produced. If we just think about how many people live in New York or in the United States and add 2 kg of waste per day, we get a crazy number. If we count with 324.000.000 we can easily calculate that a daily amount of 648.000.000 kg are produced each day, the monthly amount is 30 times this figure, that is, 9.720.000.000 kg. How much could we reduce this number if everyone was leading a more sustainable way of life? We can also estimate this figure if we take into account Rob's example: he hardly produces any waste. In 2013 when he was cycling for 104 days to draw people's attention to sustainable living, he only produced 0.9 kg waste, that is, he did not throw any waste into the rubbish bins during 3.5 months.

Of course, today's housewives do not go to the shops with paper based shopping lists if they are conscious consumers, they rather use apps that show the exact figures, how much they spent on shopping, including food. We should follow their example. In order to manage our costs we have the option to use Expense IQ Money Manager[154], which is a free application, but other apps are also available. In a few weeks', some months' time these apps will show exactly what were the categories on which we spent more than we should have, what can be left out on our next shopping trip and which items can be obtained cheaper elsewhere. This means, that after a while, if we do not wish to spend so much, the applications will encourage us to change and as the English housewife, to buy things cheaper but in better quality. In other words, not shopping in supermarkets.

Technology may help us not only in analyzing costs but also in the compilation of a caloric value based diet. Based on the appropriate amount of calories we can calculate how much food we need to buy if we are cooking lunch for a family of four. This is an efficient way to avoid someone eating extra portions, we only provide the food that is consumed in the end and no waste is produced. Eating a reasonable amount shall also be normative in cases when we cook more in order to have something for dinner as well; it is understandable that we do not want to spend our time in the kitchen cooking. In this case, however, we have to eat everything during dinner time, even if it seems boring to eat the same thing again, otherwise the food might become waste. Of course, the food can also be frozen; however, freezing food consumes energy which results in additional costs.

With the appropriate calculation we can achieve that everyone has enough to eat, lives on a healthy diet, the menu can be diversified during the whole week while no waste is produced. In the world of IoT – even if we cannot see it clearly how – our super smart phone draws up our weekly menu and our diet program if necessary and it shows us what to buy and where.

The calculation may concern the crucial question how much meat we can eat during a certain week as it is common knowledge that meat is expensive, at least in comparison to basic vegetables and fruits. However, the general consumer got used to eating meat every day, although this was not the case 100-150 years ago. And not only the developed societies would like to consume more and more meat, as economy began to develop in China and India, poorer people began to eat more meat due to globalization, since they could afford it more than before. However, if we would like to draw up a healthy diet, it shall entail the decrease of meat intake, since these diets contain more vegetables and fruits. Grilled vegetables with roast potatoes and melted cheese or a simple Minestrone soup can be really delicious. There are lots of dishes without meat on Pinterest, good ideas from the recipes of Mexican and Chinese kitchen; it is enough to browse the internet for about 10-20 minutes. If we produce our own vegetables and fruits, in a certain sense we might be forced to consume vegetable-based meals permanently: if some peppers or tomatoes and an egg-plant have ripened we must eat them before they become over-ripe and unsuitable for consumption, that is, waste. It might seem too complicated to draw up a diet in line with vegetable production but it is not that complex in practice, moreover, it makes life easier: all we have to do is to pick the vegetables in our garden and to broil them with cheese and serve them with potatoes. Fresh vegetables and fruits, picked right from the tree do not lose their nutritional value and vitamin content unlike those that are transported and stored for days then taken to the supermarkets. In addition to this, such vegetables and fruits do not contain enough minerals, trace elements or vitamins[155], thus the consumers living in developed societies have been considered as quality starvers for a long time. While 100 years ago, eating one or two peppers accounted for half of the C-vitamin dose required for your daily amount, today you would need to eat even a kilogram of pepper to be at the same standard of vitamin intake.

Due to lack of vitamin C intake it is not a miracle that we develop symptoms of flu and cold, half of society is suffering from some kind of illness. In order to cure these illnesses, consumers buy antibiotics and powders mitigating symptoms instead of eating properly – home-grown vegetables for example – and staying healthy, thus not spending a fortune on medicine treating the symptoms only. Staying healthy saves a lot of money, the money spent on medicine is money down the drain due to 'negligence', that is, waste. If you continue to buy low quality vegetables and fruits in supermarkets, you keep buying organic waste that is of hardly any use for your body and you will become sick from time to time, in spite of the fact that you try to cure yourself with medicine. This is a vicious circle where there is no doubt who has the gain and who draws the shorter straw. The consumer loses, that is for sure, the supermarkets and the pharmaceutical companies will get their profit. It is not accidental that besides the weapons industry, pharmaceutical companies and supermarket chains distributing food are the richest companies in the world. Moreover, due to the fact that there are more and more sick people, they profit the most. Do you remember the Dervaes family who organized their life based on self-sufficient production? They do not take any medicines or resort to it if it is absolutely required, instead of taking drugs they use the medicinal plants grown in their own garden. However, if there is no other chance, you have to take medicines because tolerating unnecessary pain is nothing else but waste.

Welfare societies not only face the problem of wasted food but with food packaging. Our shopping comes in countless plastic bags, producing huge amounts of rubbish and waste in the world. The bags used to serve the purpose of comfortable shopping. Had the inventors known what it meant for the planet, they would never have applied this solution, the vast majority of these plastic bags lands in water, rivers and seas and the ocean where they account for 75% of the plastic waste, according to statistics, killing lots of animals or making them sick. In order to stop this process, as of 2016 the French government put a ban on plastic bags in supermarket[156] in France. They banned their use not only in supermarkets or smaller shops but at petrol stations, pharmacies, at organic markets, thus including the entire commercial sector. The French government argued that a plastic bag is manufactured within a second on average, we use it for about 20 minutes then it goes to waste and from there to the environment and it takes 400 years to decompose. Until 2016 about 17 billion plastic bags were in commercial use, thus France largely contributed to environment pollution. And the next step? As of 1 July 2016 supermarkets are only allowed to use organic bags which are biodegradable. However, the French went even further than banning plastic bags from commercial use: during the fall of 2016 another law followed the already existing legislation. The new legislation[157] which will come into force as of 2020 only allows disposable restaurant glasses and plates to be made of biodegradable material, they banned all plastic disposables. Pack2Go Europe, the organization representing the interests of packaging companies in Brussels immediately expressed their concern stressing that there is no proof that biodegradable materials are less harmful for the environment than plastics. In addition, it is the consumers who are liable for scattering waste all around in their environment; they will think that they can throw away the waste anywhere, since it is biodegradable. In the United Kingdom[158], following the examples of Wales, Northern Ireland and Scotland no such drastic measures were introduced, the legislators tried to prevent the accumulation of waste and rubbish with other methods. Since the supermarkets have to pay 5 pennies after each plastic bag, they were forced to make their customers pay for these bags, there was a significant decrease in the purchase of plastic bags as of October 2015, in 6 months by 85%. What does it mean in figures? In half a year, only 500 million bags were bought compared to 7 billion. This is a result that we can be proud of, however, plastic is still present in the packaging industry, in everyday commercial use, typically in the form of PET bottles, plastic foils and other packaging tools. Nevertheless, it is a reassuring fact that there are more and more articles and news in the media concerning the invention of alternative packaging materials, including an edible packaging foil[159] used for packaging cheese, meat and fruit instead of plastic.

Without packaging

The idea of zero waste was conceived in California during the 70s, by the creation of Zero Waste Systems Inc.[160] founded by Paul Palmer. Given the name of the company, a completely new philosophy spread in economy, business and society and it created the notion of a home without waste. Palmer and his followers were convinced that though it might seem difficult to achieve, it was possible to live a waste-free life, do our shopping and manage a household without waste. Today with the help of the internet, YouTube, on experts' blogs and books we can get information required to reach this objective, just to mention one example: Bea Jonhson[161]. Bea's educational videos can be viewed by anyone and the knowledge related to waste-free household, shopping can be mastered.

Nowadays there are shops where you can buy food ingredients without packaging,
in Berlin, Germany or several towns and cities of France[162] and in the United States just as well as in the UK. Although results are reassuring, the ideal state of producing no waste after shopping is an objective we still have to work on. Unfortunately, average consumers will continue obtaining their food in supermarkets, so where legislator do

173

not take the necessary legal measures to ban the disposal of food into garbage bins or the use of disposable plastic bags, all we are left with is wastefulness. Except for cases when the consumer becomes a conscious shopper as we pointed out above, drawing up a diet, obtaining food from the countryside and regional community agriculture, farming. In these cases there is no need for plastic bags or packaging, only two boxes. In one of the boxes the goods arrive, the other box goes back empty to obtain the next portion of food. The box is made of wood or cardboard, both of these materials are biodegradable, therefore sure to decompose at the end of its life-cycle.

If there are farmer's markets around our place of residence, of course we can obtain the goods there as well; however, this may be more expensive than products transported from rural agricultural units. The advantage is that we can buy food from there at any time. In this case we can look for the baskets used by our great grandmas, an optimal solution for transporting potatoes and apples at the same time. Berries, such as raspberries or blueberries can also be taken home in appropriate boxes; we should stick to this transport solution, although the producers might ask you why you do not want a plastic bag. In these cases no waste is produced since there are no packaging materials. Even conscious consumers have to buy some products in supermarkets, such as coffee, cocoa, bananas or rice, even if the amount of waste is scarce, some might be produced. Nevertheless, this amount is negligible if we compare to the huge amounts accumulated by the average consumer each year, this is a sufficient result in itself. A great result since a zero waste home is never exactly zero, always just converging to zero. With such a small amount of waste, however, the waste management industry can easily cope, rather than huge piles of waste. Another advantage is that it does not place an extra burden on the environment, and technological development will soon answer the question when all plastic materials will be replaced by organic and biodegradable ones. The future that we thought was a faraway dream is no longer so distant, it is a vital question since plastic is made of mineral oil, a raw material that we are running out of all around the world, agricultural areas are also exhausted, as a consequence of large-scale agricultural collapse, this triggers the fall of trade through big supermarket chains. At that time we will see the upheaval of small-scale agriculture, we will see the advantage of having a plot of land, a farmers' market and community farming that provides sufficient amount of vegetables and fruits for people through sustainable production.

Physical activity, diet and changes in our lifestyle

In 2014, it was a scientific sensation, a breakthrough when Austrian scientists discovered that cells storing fat could be transformed into cells burning fat. This would have meant that overweight people could get rid of the fat that accumulated in their bodies throughout the years without any physical activity. According to the researcher, Marcel Scheidler[163], due to unnecessary fat half of the Austrian people are overweight that leads to several illnesses, among others, diabetes. However, if becoming overweight could be eliminated, we would not have to calculate with the risk of diabetes and other diseases, so many people would not die so early. Unfortunately, we have not heard anything about the scientists' discovery, whereas this 'treatment' would do good to welfare states' consumers, since obesity has been an epidemic for a long time. An epidemic that we could fight with appropriate diet and a strict regime, however, people do the opposite, overeat and get sick, then finally die too early.

How much does the diet cost? It depends on how much you spend on it but let's look at the market related to this, what are the figures. In 2013, in the United States, if we take into account the value of books on diet, food supplements and operations we can calculate with an industry of 20 billion dollars. There are more than 300 million people living in the United States, out of which 108 million are on diet, the price of operations aimed at decreasing the stomach capacity is between 11.5 and 26 thousand dollars. These data give you an overview about the current state of welfare societies and the industry that is built around diets. The money that people spend on diets, obtaining books on how to lose weight and on pills could be saved if everyone was conscious about daily eating habits. Nevertheless, the average consumers find it difficult to follow the healthy path.

They find it difficult to live a healthy life in spite of the fact that losing weight is even more complicated. The American group of researchers made the same discovery writing in the New England Journal of Medicine[164] in 2016: a diet shall not be started on the very first day of the year but during the preceding months as well, before Thanksgiving. The same applies to retaining our ideal body weight. At these times of the year consumers can put on weight by consuming even 7-10,000 calories a day, which is more difficult to get rid of later on. Conscious behavior and planned consumption helps consumers resist the temptation. According to the findings of the research group, only 66 days[165] are enough to internalize and master these behavior patterns and turn them into habits. We will have optimal weight and be healthy, let alone the amount of money that we are not wasting but sparing compared to overweight people by avoiding overeating and not spending any money on diets.

Eating habits and being overweight are closely interrelated, this is well-known just as well as the fact that physical activity helps us get rid of unnecessary weight, but this is not the only reason why doing sports is good for you. It is a good activity, helps get rid of stress, a sort of relaxation, makes us feel refreshed. There are many sports, from swimming to fitness trainings, aerobics and body building, if we do not wish to spend much on entry fees to swimming pools or gyms, running and biking can also be useful. Starting to train by running or biking seems easy for many of us, but for those who have not practiced any sports for years now, it is not that easy. In order to avoid harmful consequences and to see the required results, it is worth consulting a doctor or a nutritionist, since most of the consumers who do not see any changes within a short period of time will cease the activity. Of course, once again it is incorrect mentality, greed and avarice that dominates since the majority of people on a diet intend to lose weight immediately, within days, and when they face the fact that losing weight does not happen from one day to the next, give it up, not seeing the 'gain' in the process. The experts explain that long-term success lies in slow slimming, this is the only way to avoid putting on the extra weight again, and our body has to get used to the new state which requires time. Many people understand only when they have started a diet that it is much more than trying to lose some weight, a complete change in their lifestyle and dietary habits is a program that has long term objectives. Losing the extra weight is half of the success story; the other half is trying to keep our optimal weight and to retain our health.

In the absence of useful information we could still start a diet, but if the diet is not successful, for example we gain weight within a short, while we did not do anything else but wasted a lot of money, time and invested energy, that is, we did not produce anything else but waste.

The waste that we put on can be burned if we keep in mind how many calories can be burnt by appropriate physical activity, but it is still better if we do not produce this waste at all, since we know that the best waste is the waste that has not even been produced. If we got through a diet, that is half success, some months are sufficient to experience when physical activity has to be started with the specific purpose of losing weight.

Shall we eat insects?

In the 20th century, there was a huge population growth, there have never been so many people living on our planet. A Hungarian professor, Dr. István Láng[166] started his presentation at a conference a few years ago by saying that at the time of his birth, at the beginning of the 30s, there were only 2 billion people on the Earth, but this figure shall be multiplied by 7 to calculate the number of the population. By 2050, we shall calculate with a rise of 9 times, and by 2100 with 12 times. These numbers make it evident that our planet is overpopulated and this trend would not be changed or reversed by a pandemic or another world war as some would think, at least there was a comprehensive study[167] about it in 2014 written by Corey J. A. Bradshaw and Barry W. Brook, American researchers, in the PNAS journal of the US Academy of Sciences. It is interesting and at the same time surprising that the world became so overpopulated during this century, how this immense population can be supplied with sufficient amount of food, it is a complex issue, how the nutrition of so many people can be solved with only vegetables and animal protein. It is evident that we have to look for alternative solutions; researchers argue that a diet based on insects can be a viable solution, either for human consumption or for animal fodder. It is not an accidental choice to use insects as food ingredient, since insects and bugs have been part of everyday diet in Asia, Latin America and Africa as well. In developed societies there is a general phobia related to insects, however, according to a dietitian, Daniella Martin[168], we have to change our attitude, since if welfare states would like to follow a sustainable path in nutrition as well; changing completely unsustainable large-scale agricultural patterns shall include a new diet, too. This might also mean that we can produce not only plants in our garden, but breed insects, too, producing such food is much cheaper and means less waste than producing animal protein (meat), which requires lots of resources.

If anyone hears the information that we are going to eat insects, one tends to think of insects stabbed on a barbecue pitch, however, this is not the case, this will not be the substantial ingredient in our diet. Insects will provide the food ingredient for flour; some sorts are in commercial use already. We can bake meatloaf or cakes of the flour, a venturesome journalist has tried some of them. According to Catherine Lamb[169], the cakes made of silkworms reminded her of drawers that have not been used for a long time, but it tasted sweet like aspartame. The cakes made of scorpion flour had a bit of a tinge, but it was not disturbing, I could eat it. The sweets made of cricket flour smelled like walnuts, its taste proved to be quite average. The journalist drew the conclusion that the cricket flour can become a basic food ingredient, but the other two types of flour will possibly be consumed by people on a permanent basis. Cricket flour can be used to make chocolate, this idea was conceived in the minds of Gabi Lewis and Greg Sewitz some years ago and they founded a company with the name Exo100[170] to distribute the chocolate. They stated that insects contained 20 times more protein than cattle, at the same time they release 80 times less methane, thus the use of raw material is much more environmentally friendly than breeding animals for which even the fodder has to be produced.

Cosmetics and detergents

In relation to water consumption we stressed the importance of preparing our own soap for example, since several hygiene products or cosmetics may contain chemicals that can harm our health as in case of antibacterial soaps. If we want to make sure and we do not want to let in any chemicals in our household, we can buy bio products, but they are very expensive, and in addition to this, they come in plastic bottles, containers, thus we produce waste again, so if we want to avoid this situation or if we wish to obtain the products cheaper, we have to produce our own cosmetics and detergents. Of course, everyone starts by buying these products in the shop whose packaging is not disposable; it can be retained for further use later on. For example, a deo roll-on or pump deodorant dispenser can come in handy if they are refillable, it shall not end as waste, this we cannot substitute with our own tool. We can find a substitute for a plastic shampoo or liquid detergent containers, smaller or bigger glasses can serve the same purpose.

On the internet, several videos and blog comments can be read with recipes describing and presenting the preparation of cosmetics and detergents, thus anyone can choose what they like and can 'produce' them at home on a regular basis. If you have a calculator and you register how much you spent on each detergent during a period of 2-3 months and compared to this how much it costs to achieve the same objective with sustainable cleansing materials, you may soon discover that home-made cosmetics are generally cheaper than the ones bought in the shop, of course it depends on the kind of detergent and from where we can obtain the basic ingredients. If we can produce a part of these ingredients, because we produce a certain medicinal plant in our garden, the product is partly available free of charge, but it is cheaper if it is available locally and is not imported.

Many of us hear that the products in commercial use contain lots of chemicals and that they can harm our health, thus they would be ready and willing to use other types of cosmetics, but they do not know where to start. Katie Wells, known as Wellness Mama[171] – she is a distributor of e-book and publishes her posts on a regular basis – can help us: she not only demonstrates how to start manufacturing our own home-made cosmetics and other detergents, but she also makes available chemical-free recipes that we can produce ourselves. In one of her videos[172], she presents how we can save lots of time and money by producing our own products instead of buying them in shops, which means that Katie kills two birds with one stone. She not only makes her home healthier, but cheaper as well. Besides, her household does not produce any significant amount of waste, which is much less than the quantity produced in the case when shopping is done at stores.

It is an interesting coincidence if a housewife prepares the soaps out of home waste, namely out of used vegetable oil[173]. Even an enterprise can grow out of a good idea, Burt Shavitznak[174], a photographer living in New York, had such a success story. He got bored with city life, left society and he started a new life in the countryside as a hippy. Since he loved beekeeping, he began to sell honey on the local market and he used the remaining material for preparing hand creams, lip balms and furniture waxes. All this happened by accident, as Burt met his business partner, Roxanne Quimby while hitchhiking, she was the woman who gave him the idea of using the accumulated beeswax and to prepare and sell cosmetics. Burt's Bees products gained popularity in the States, thus our hero and his business partners became rich within a few years' time and the company was finally bought up by

Clorox for 935 million dollars in 2007. It is interesting that, although Burt established a company worth almost 1 billion dollars, he was not interested in business and profit, he continued to live in the countryside and did not do anything else but beekeeping and playing with his dogs, from time to time peeing circles in the white snow. He could afford to live alone, no one spoke badly of him.

Of course, we cannot produce all our cosmetics and household items; one of them is toilet paper.

WASHING AND WASHING UP, CLEANING OF THE HOUSE

Washing

When American housewives were reading about shirts designed by an American company in 2013 that could be worn for about 100 days without getting dirty or smelly, many of them were immediately interested, since they all had one important question to ask. You don't need to wash or iron this item at all? This would be the dream of American housewives? Of course we can wash it, however, the Wool and Prince[175] startup company that has developed it, stressed the importance of treating it with care. Anyway, you do not need to iron it, it does not crease. Naturally, the housewives were rather interested in quitting their tiresome job if they buy such a shirt from the company that became famous all of a sudden at Kickstarter, we thought right about how good it is for the environment and the little energy it requires, not to mention the little waste that is produced during the wear of such an item if it only has to be washed four times a year. We have to add, however, that no one will wear the same shirt for 100 days; it means that you do not have to wash it for years if we suppose that the web-shop of the company offers not only one product, but a whole collection. Might it be reasonable to buy several shirts, T-shirts or underwear from the company's web-shop if the 'operational costs' of the product are much lower than in case of traditional ones? Anyone can calculate or estimate it if they know the price of an average shirt, the amount of money it requires to wash and to iron it and how many times you have to do this each year. Nevertheless, if you make a decision, you should first try the product.

As for why is it worth buying an item that we can wear for years or even two decades and how many of these do you need to live a comfortable life, you should see the Clothing and wardrobe subchapter which will be available soon. The most important thing about clothing is that it should be for life, tolerate tear and wear, it is pointless to buy more and more items because you bought bad quality items. You should only buy clothes that do not lose their color or flexibility after washing. For this, we have to be aware exactly what and how we shall wash in order to keep it in good condition.

It might be evident that we buy several items of the same type, only their color differs, for summer some T-shirts, for winter warm underwear. This might be a model behavior for our family members, we can encourage them to wear the same sort of clothes, thus during the same period of time the clothes can accumulate which can be washed according to the same standards, that is, saving energy. When I discovered that despite the messages of advertisements, my T-shirts and underwear made of the same material can be washed in cold tapwater, I not only saved energy, but also managed to keep the color of these items by not washing them at 30 or 40 degrees. I saved a lot of money by avoiding the purchase of the same quality T-shirt, since it lost its color after the first wash.

Washing depends on lots of factors: whether we have children, the type of work we do, whether we are allergic to detergents and softeners, the first decision we have to make is whether we need a washing machine or not. In the country it is a bit more complicated, but in cities we have popular networks where we can take our clothes, detergent and softener and we are ready to wash. The washing machines operated in self-service laundries run each day of the week, well exploited while our machines at home are not at all. Laundries seem to offer a more environmentally friendly solution, since in this case you do not need to buy a machine for yourself; however, you have to calculate before you make a decision. Especially when you plan to buy an absolutely environmentally friendly washing machine, you have to compare its operational costs to the fee of a laundry. You have to take into account the hours of operation and the guarantee period. Of course, you should not buy a machine that goes wrong after the operational hours defined. Before purchasing the machine you have to check the tests available on the internet, you have to view the opinions and postings related to this topic, check users' experiences and to take into account the users' opinion instead of the seller's. The sellers are only interested in selling the product, they have their script and they have their answer to each of your questions.

Smart washing machines

When purchasing a washing machine, it is worth taking into consideration that within a few years' time there will be a wide range of smart washing machines to choose from. Nevertheless, they will be much more expensive than the original ones, though they can be remote controlled through the internet, they can only do one washing once, not more, for more washing cycles you have to be at home and reload the machine. For the time being we cannot really see the advantage of the already available smart washing machines. If we compare this function to the remote controlled heating regulation, namely that we can pre-set the heating in our house from our smart phone half an hour before we get home, thus the house has a pleasant temperature by the time we get home and we can immediately see the difference. Moreover, technically more complicated devices can go wrong much easier or contamination by pests, therefore it is worth organizing our life in such a way that we get the washing over with on time.

Before drying machines appeared on the market, housewives used to dream about such an appliance, of course lots of time can be saved by avoiding the need to hang out and dry clothes. This is especially true for winter, clothes dry slower and heating is needed. It is a good question whether it is worth buying a separate drying machine and not a hybrid one where the drying function is integrated in one machine. The choice is yours, according to experts' opinion it is better to have a separate drying machine if the customer can afford it, these products are relatively expensive and they occupy lots of space, most of the apartments do not have the layout for so many appliances. When I was asking laundry employees about drying machines, the majority of them said that sunshine was better. Wherever possible, it is worth making use of natural energy, it is for free, we only need a clothesline and we do not need to spend so much for a machine. In the winter we do not have sunshine, in vain do we wait for it, and where we do not have a chance to dry clothes outside, a clothesline that can be pulled up may be the optimal solution[176] even in the bathroom if we keep the washing machine there. A clothesline that can be pulled up was very popular among older generations; our grandmas loved it, by now it has almost completely disappeared. Nevertheless, if we decide to go for one, we can buy it in shops and manufacture it at home, it is not a complex task. If this simple device can be installed somewhere in the flat, we not only profit from saving space but we also make use of the heating. There are other alternatives than buying an expensive drying machine or a hybrid one; we only have to think about how to spare the costs, still finding an optimal solution in our household.

The question is not only about whether we should buy a washing or drying machine, it also concerns our detergent and softener, shall we buy them in the supermarket or shall we produce our own. If we do not want to use any chemicals and do not wish to spend a fortune on organic products, we have to make our own cleaning substances. Fortunately, there are lots of webpages on how to make washing powders and softeners at home, Matt and Betsy Jabs have even written a book[177] on the topic, how much money we can save by homemade detergents. We most frequently use washing nuts, washing soda or soap; we hardly use softeners since these products perfume the clothes. If we still need the softener, it is worth trying the simplest one. All we need is 1 dl of washing soda, 1 dl vinegar, 1 dl water, 6 drops of citrus oil and we have a nice softener with the desired effect, but we can substitute citrus oil with lavender or other fragrances.

We would not think but there is a lot of information on the internet as for how to do our washing in a sustainable way. It is worth browsing, here are some tips and advice that shall include but not limited to the substantial definitions and solutions and what shall be avoided.

Some tips, a non-exhaustive list

1. Natural versions: We can learn a lot from our grandmas, their generation did not use so much detergent and softeners, whiteners, though the clothes were clean at that time, too. The natural version of the detergents currently available in supermarkets can be downloaded from the internet, if we have time we can make them at home. Obtaining the ingredients is a bit more complex. It is not only our grandmothers from whom we can learn, but we have to make a little investigation about the materials that can be obtained at low cost in order to make our own detergent and if necessary, our

own softener. It is worth knowing the softness of the local tap water, whether we need a water softener for 'hard' water.

2. Frequent mistakes and disasters: If possible we should not learn from our mistakes. Selecting the clothes according to colors shall be a basic principle, though many families might have experienced the consequence of a red item being washed together with light colors.

These problems can be avoided, they can be traced back to delegating washing to a man or a teenage child, we should not suppose that they know how to do this task. Even if it requires more time, it is better to explain and demonstrate to them what and how shall be washed, otherwise a disaster might happen if they want to do the washing alone, we can throw the clothes right to the bin afterwards. Men tend to think generally that automatic washing machines are miraculous appliances that make anything clean and they only have to set the appropriate program. Finally, when they face the shrunken or pinkish white clothes they discover that more patience, care and expertise are needed for washing. Just the same, it has to be explained to them that paper tissues shall be removed from pockets, why shall we wash white with white or the same colors together, why shall we turn jeans inside out, etc. It is worth informing them about the frequency of washing: towels and pajama shall be washed every fifth week, sheets and linen every second week, jeans after the fifth occasion, swimming suits after each use.

3. Soaking: In case of stains that are difficult to remove the clothes shall be soaked, so that the washing program requiring much energy can be avoided, though many people expect washing program to be efficient alone. It is not at all sure, however, that the clothes will be clean after just one washing, the average consumer throws these clothes away and they end up in the bin. Depending on the nature of the stain (due to beetroots, mustard, chocolate or fat) we shall find

the optimal solution on the internet, how to remove it, we shall not experiment. We rarely manage to achieve the objective ourselves, if the cleaning is unsuccessful, these textiles go to waste.

4. Clothes can be washed by a washing soap or washing soda perfectly; another advantage is that they are environmentally friendly and not at all expensive, unlike popular products containing phosphate available in supermarkets.

5. Cleaning: The washing machine shall be cleaned regularly, for which the best and cheapest solution is vinegar. Vinegar dissolves scale and the accumulated detergent as well; in addition, you do not have to spend money on softeners. If the machine is not used, you have to leave its door or its lid open so that it can dry.

6. Quantity and energy: We should follow the instructions specified in case of each program. If we wash a smaller quantity, we waste water and energy, while if we wash a bigger quantity than specified, the effectiveness of washing deteriorates. Everyone has an optimal temperature for washing, at 30 or 40 degrees cleaning can be optimal, you do not need to use pre-heated water of 60 degrees for every wash. Despite misconceptions, it is not the turning of the drum that consumes the most energy, but heating up the water used for washing. You can read the care instructions on any items, whether they can be washed in a washing machine and at what temperature.

Washing up

Just in case of shaving, it is a common sight in some households to do the washing up by running tap water[178], placing an immense burden on the environment and wasting lots of money. Sustainable washing up methods help you save lots of water and money, not much information is required, you only have to follow some basic rules.

First and foremost you have to use every drop of water. You might have lots of dirty dishes and pots after cooking, including cutlery; it is worth soaking them in water. Nothing else is needed, only one part of the sink or a big bowl, you need to fill it with water and sodium bicarbonate[179]. These substances will do their work, dissolve the dirt, thus it can be easily removed. While doing the washing up, you have to respect the order! First, less contaminated kitchen tools will be washed after soaking, typically cups and glasses, spoons, etc. Then you need to place the dirtier bowls which have to be soaked for a longer period of time. After the stains and food remains have become loose, they can be washed.

For rinsing you should use a perlator[180] which helps you reduce water consumption significantly. Recently, a Swedish company has developed a device that is capable of sparing 98% of water according to the video. [181] What does it mean in numbers? The perlator that costs 49 euros (53 dollars), that is capable of reducing water consumption from 8-12 liters to 0.18. Of course, cheaper tools are also available, and you can save up to 50-70% with them.

The use of home-made washing up liquids is effective since it is sustainable and it does not harm our hands and health. At the same time it is cheaper than other products available in the shops. Many people use washing soda, a substance that was very popular in our grandmas' time. If we pour 3 tablespoons of washing soda in an empty bottle, pour warm water on it and then shake it well, we get an ideal washing up liquid. Of course, there are several webpages which report about home-made washing up liquids, for example the products of Matt and Betsy we can chose from.[182]

Washing up by hand or a dishwasher?

A few years, decades ago when the use of dishwashers became widespread, the first tests appeared to examine which solution was more cost-effective, washing up by hand or using a dishwasher. There are no calculations which can be considered authentic in this respect, but the objective of the manufacturers was to make tiresome housework more comfortable rather than making dishwashing more cost-effective. Washing up is a time-consuming and dirty activity; the person doing it shall lean forward, which often causes a backache. For this reason, the manufacturers offered a great solution to a tiresome problem, success was a foregone conclusion, just as well as the fact that the user would never get his money's worth if we looked at the costs of purchasing and operating. However, if we looked at the time that is saved – except for loading in the dishes and taking them out of the machine - for many it would be worth investing in a smaller machine worth a few hundred dollars. It is an important question which machines are more useful, once we decide to buy one. Machines saving water are more expensive, but their operation does not cost as much as that of traditional machines, first we have to examine if the brand often requires servicing and maintenance, for how many hours it can be operated and then we can examine the amount of water and electricity that it is capable of saving.

Similarly, in case of washing up, washing up liquids and tablets can also be substituted by home-made products.

Cleaning

Here we could have made reference to point 7 related to washing as an advice, since the grey water remaining after washing , can be very useful if we can collect it and use it for washing the floor. Otherwise we can pour it down the toilet, so we can use it for other purposes. For these activities we shall not waste drinking water, water that we otherwise pay for.

However, sustainable and cost-effective cleaning does not start here, but with dimensions. If the flat or apartment is small, you don't really need to clean it, unlike in case of a big house having a floor space of about 200 m² or even more, where average Americans live. In order to keep clean such a huge house, you need to hire someone, a cleaner, this entails a regular monthly cost, depending on how many times the service is needed. The smaller the flat, the lower the costs, especially if we are able to clean the house ourselves. In this case we do not need to spend money on a cleaner. Do you remember Dee Williams and the cabin houses? He made a very snappy statement in his book entitled The Big Tiny: A Built-It-Myself Memoir[183] about the problems related to the maintenance of a big house and the simplicity and cost-effectiveness of a smaller one.

Cleaning is a great business all around the world, one example for that is the German startup based on share economy which began to grow all of a sudden. Helpling[184] profited from the idea of sending a cleaner at any time, for example after a party, while cleaners are generally available at a set time, for example once or twice a week.

Not only big companies can be successful in business, one good example for that is the enterprise of IleneScoratow named Another Mother[185] started in January 2014. The clients of the enterprise are university students, the enterprise derives its name from here, since Scoratow does the same as any mothers who have to look after their kids too, busy with studying – shopping, cleaning and washing for them.

If we prepare the products needed for cleaning, we can save significant amounts of money compared to supermarket choices. This applies to toilet fresheners and blocks as well, if they are required at all. Our grandmothers used toilets without these for years, without being at a disadvantage. The same is true for detergents, which are capable to kill bacteria under the fringe of the toilet. All these substances were invented by people working in the chemical industry and skilled marketing personnel managed to sell them, producing lots of plastic waste, let alone the amount of chemicals contaminating sewage and waters. If you think about how many such tools are used in your household, you can find other ones.

We should constantly keep cleaning fluids in the toilet, and it is worth watching the video again, which shows how to refill the empty plastic container of the previously bought detergent with homemade cleaning fluid.[186]

UNNECESSARY OBJECTS IN THE HOUSEHOLD

Aiming at the sufficient minimum

The emphasis is not only on choosing the right house, organizing self-sufficiency and a healthy diet it we aim at spending less than the great average, but on how many assets and tools we own and fill our household. You should remember Andrew Hyde[187], who said that even if we are travelling, we only need 15 basic objects? It might sound as an exaggeration, but aiming at the sufficient minimum shall be kept as a principle if we would like to organize our life or make a choice about buying another object in our household. We can draw up a simple comparison demonstrating how average citizens tend to buy things without previous planning and how many useless objects and junks they accumulate where they live. If you look at your own living space and the video of Bea Johnson's[188] house, you will immediately spot the difference. Bea's house seems spacious and orderly, since she only stores the absolute minimum, the objects she and her family definitely need every day, while the living space of the average consumer seems to resemble a lumber-room, rather than a living space where one actually likes to be. Of course, the reason for this is that the average consumer tends to buy objects that they only use or wear only once or never. These tools generally land in the lumber-room, and later on when the owner dies they are thrown away.

The market of once used or almost futile objects is huge; this is justified by the fact that there are company owners such as Kevin Harrington[189]. Besides selling usable kitchen and household equipment, Kevin sold useless things as well, and he was very successful.

He started his teleshop in the 80s, which proved to be a great business, since the fortune of the businessman amounted to 450 million dollars. He sold a 360 degree dog cleaner, hair spray covering baldness, towels that can be worn as dresses, as well as facial muscle strengthener, singing toothbrush or golf clubs into which you could even pee. It is difficult to stop laughing when you watch these videos on YouTube, however, people bought them, otherwise Harrington would not have been able to sell them.

Clothes and our wardrobe

It is not a difficult task to select the clothes for Mark Zuckenberg, in general he wears the same sort of clothes, similarly to a woman who wears the same style of costumes when going to work each day, as the founder of Facebook. Melinda Kahl[190] does not have to wear a uniform at her workplace; she was the one who decided to wear the same clothes each day. Her behavior seemed strange at first, but there is a sort of social criticism behind it. Melinda got bored with the tiresome ceremony of dressing up each day, with selecting different clothes each day, having to please his boss and colleagues and even business partners, so she decided to opt for a uniform that was acceptable for all of them, she bought a few of the same kind and she has been using it ever since. Of course, she does not wear the same clothes each day of the year, she has diverse sets of clothes, however, the items of these sets are exactly the same. Thanks to this strange habit, the young woman does not have to spend her free time with strolling around in boutiques shopping, constantly planning what to wear and catch discount and sale periods, that is, she got rid of the constraints of consumption. It is obvious that she has much more free time as a consequence, it is a positive outcome, and she has more money because her wardrobe is not full of useless items, with clothes going to the lumber-room. The young woman was not so much motivated by avoiding waste to adopt this seemingly 'strange' behavior, but rather by the objective that she should be assessed rather by her work and not her appearance at her workplace. In spite of all this, her behavior also changed unwittingly, she is a good example for those who decided to turn their back on the constantly changing demands of the world of fashion, who would like to save money spent on clothes, at the same time wishing to appear in a few, comfortable set of clothes. Either for their workplace or for home wear.

For those working from home – and there will be more and more such employees in the world of IoT - a limited set of clothes will be sufficient, it might sound strange but pleasant that pajamas or leisure-wear will be sufficient, since they are never going to meet their bosses, and just very rarely with colleagues, they won't see each other, maybe through skype. This sort of lifestyle makes it possible to create a set of similar clothes for which you do not have to spend so much and which is easier to wash. By the time they are 20 or 30, people have a significant collection, and there are some items they have never worn, or just on a few occasions, nothing else but old-fashioned belongings no longer used, practically waste. This sort of wasting behavior, in spite of the fact that we could make more conscious shopping decisions, will still be present in welfare states, since an American family spends 1700 dollars on clothes in general[191], however, they throw 30 kg of clothes to the garbage within this period of time[192]. This figure makes you think, what is this wasteful behavior good for, however, until the majority of people cannot handle their money and spend it on useful things, that is, they spend more on a monthly basis than what they earn, we presume that the same trend will prevail, since the difference will be covered by bank loans and they do not think that it is a big problem if they live their whole lives in debt. Surveys seem to support this theory[193], they show that 43% of American households spends more than what they earn, 52% of employees live from month to month, and 42% of people do not have savings sufficient to cover three months' expenses.

As for clothing, this means that many consumers who buy clothes, partly resort to loans when shopping, then after contributing to the banks' and supermarkets' profit, after a short period of wear they throw the old-fashioned items into the bin that they were craving for so much. This is how valuable clothes become useless trash and how the average consumer becomes a life-long debtor. We do not know exactly, how many clothes are required by those working from home. Presumably much less than those who go to their workplaces each day like Melinda Kahl, only in sets according to the last fashion trend, trying to look perfect.

How to quit the bad habit of constant shopping?

What happens when someone decides not to buy any clothes for a year? Basically nothing, it is not the end of the world. This is what we can read in Sarah Lazarovic's book, A Bunch of Pretty Things I Did Not Buy[194], where the author points out that the average consumers buy many clothes during a year that they do not wear and do not need at all. According to Sarah, shopping is a psychological process, the consumer makes emotional decisions, since it is impossible not to be influenced by the overwhelming visual impulses of advertisements suggesting that the consumer absolutely needs this or that product, at any rate. In vain do they have a sense of guilt afterwards, consumers will 'succumb to the temptation' over and over again.

However, conscious shopping is a method by which the process becomes reversible; those who do not make irrational shopping choices will not spend superfluous amounts. They will not need a bank loan for their spending, thus the consumer will benefit, while the bank and the supermarket will not. In case if you try to track the records of the money you spent on clothes with the help of apps mentioned above, you can see the difference and the exact amount that you can save. Facts are difficult to accept, in half a year's or a year's time we can see how our balance is improving as a result of not financing our shopping, and the bank will be forced not to give us a loan for these things.

Let's combine pleasant with useful

After a while, the process might come to a halt when we only buy the most important clothes for ourselves, especially when we begin to save money not only during our shopping trips, but in other walks of life. For example, if we do not want to heat our apartment or house during the winter – supposing that we are at home 24 hours a day – we need to buy some clothes (in case if we did not have any before) to keep us warm during unheated hours or periods. Such warm clothing, for example a polar jumper may give us a warm, cozy feeling that is what it was designed for, it is worth buying several similar items, since we will wear them for many years, depending on how often we wear and wash them.

The long-term objective is that the clothes shall serve us for at least 10 years

The long-term objective is to have clothing that fulfils this expectation; we shall be able to wear them for about 10 years, similarly to our sport clothes. Nevertheless, we shall not buy them at the same time, conscious shopping also includes austerity. If we know that polar jumpers will be offered for sale during the spring period, further items shall be bought then or if we have vouchers, we shall use them, the most important thing is that on the second or third occasion we shall get a reasonable price if possible.

We can demonstrate this by our own example, too. When we moved to the countryside, we bought a polar jumper which cost 10 dollars instead of 27, fortunately, we were in the middle of the spring sale period and no one needed such item at that time. Unfortunately, we could not buy more of the same kind, there were just some left, and we were facing the problem that these polar jumpers were not indicated in the web shop of the supermarket. The same jumpers cost 27 dollars at the end of September, and though there were some in the sports shop, they ran out of stocks quickly. Since we needed some more of these items, unwillingly we had to pay this amount, but during the springtime when they are offered at sale prices we will definitely buy some, due to frequent use they need to be washed often, so they tend to wear. However, this was not the only underlying reason to buy more. We do not need to burn so much wood, because owing to these warm clothes we are not so cold, we only heat the living area to 64-66°F.

This way we could save and spare one quarter of the wood compared to if we heated up the living space to 68-71 °F. In many cases,

199

especially if meteorology forecasts cold weather, we leave the polar jumpers on us, we sleep in them, moreover, our blankets are also made of this material in order to retain the most body heat possible. Depending on how cold the nights are, we are covering ourselves with 2-4 blankets, which makes it possible to sleep really well even after days spent with tough work.

This is of course also due to the fact that the heat insulation of the house is perfect, thus the temperature does not get colder than 62 °F. We became conscious consumers about 20 years ago, thus we are still wearing the same short and long sleeved T-shirts (100% cotton) that we bought at that time, and we could presume that they would last another 10-15 years at least. At the time we bought them with the intention of them being suitable for something if not streetwear, for example for home use, as well as gardening or doing sports. Of course, we bought some items that did not come up to our expectations, before they became shabby we gave them to charity organizations supporting the poor or sold them at garage sales or simply changed them for something else. In spite of all this, each of us has an own collection of 40-50 items, including underwear that are constantly used on a yearly basis. Everything has its own function; we bought about half of our wardrobe items at least 10 years ago. Of course, polar jumpers can come in handy when we are chopping wood for heating or move around the village. The villagers are not shocked by seeing us going around in the same clothes, similarly to Melinda's case at her workplace.

If we compare conscious shopping with ordering items from the internet, that is, impulse shopping, because we fell in love with an item on seeing it popping up with an advertisement, we can immediately see the difference between wardrobes. Similarly to the bank account statements, where we can immediately trace which shops did the consumer opt for in the last 10 years when buying clothes. If I add that we have had the habit of shopping in second hand shops, on average spending 2 or 3 dollars on practically new shirts, T-shirts, pullovers and trousers, the balance will show an even greater difference. If you decide to buy your clothes in second hand shops, it is worth looking at the calendar when the new stocks arrive and grab the opportunity to go to the shop at this time since clever customers and retailers pick the best items, later on we have a limited choice with the same items.

There is a huge business opportunity in the trading of used clothing, this is obvious, and the case of Julie Wainwright[195] demonstrates this, though in a bit more different context. The American businesswoman discovered that she could obtain luxury items from stars and celebrities if they do not wish to wear them anymore and sell these items at a higher price. After her discovery, she founded a company, applied a working business model, she opened a place where she received these items, that is, she had the items sent to her and bought the clothes there, later on she sold the clothes through a web-shop and delivered them to customers. Julie worked with a very good margin, she could buy some of the items 30-40% cheaper than the original price, then she was able to sell them at a higher price. This was not the only surprising fact for her when she started her successful business but seeing so many people trying to sell the items that they got bored with. The startup renamed RealReal became a really successful enterprise, further specialized in selling luxury jewelry, watches and works of art, working with several hundreds of employees, including 55 'luxury managers' assigned with the procurement of luxury items in 20 cities. Julie has become a millionaire, of course. It is not only Julie who can profit from selling other people's clothes that they got bored with. Laura Rose[196], a student at an English University got fed up with not being able to pay her studies and not being able to afford a living, so she decided to change her life and obtain a reasonable income. First she sold her own unused clothes on eBay at a very good price, and then she began to sell her friends' clothes, again at a very good price. After a while she had a problem with the supply, the 23-year-old student contacted Chinese wholesalers to order cheap products and sell them with a good margin. Laura, at the time when the magazines wrote about her success, earned 30 thousand pounds thanks to her simple business model, and while her peers were doing some student job for little money, she went on holidays several times. It is worth trying, those who can, are successful.

Laura became rich by selling others' clothes; she did not earn money by selling her own clothes she had previously bought for herself. However, the business bred profit for everyone in some way or another, and a lot for Laura, and the clothes at the back of the wardrobe started their new lives. We can just hope that these items were bought by conscious customers and they did not end up in another wardrobe or in the garbage bin.

Self-training

We can read several articles on conscious shopping, in internet posts or on webpages operated by civil organizations dedicated to sustainability or environmental protection[197] (there should be some references, see the footnote!).

It is worth browsing these, since the example with the above mentioned polar jumper can be a unique example and though it contains eternal truths, it is not at all sure that it can be applied in everyone's case. However, on these webpages we can read about examples which we can make use of. There are some principles which we shall consider, such as: the more expensive products might be cheaper sometimes, we should not forget that if a more expensive, better quality product can be used for 20 years, it is sure that we have to choose this product, instead of buying more of another one that is cheaper but worse quality, that cannot be used for more than one or two years. We can further develop this principle, it is essential to become a conscious consumer, but also to train ourselves and develop our knowledge further. If we were considering to buy a product about which do not have sufficient testing or information available on the internet, we should contact the manufacturer or the supermarket selling the product, thus if we need several responses at the same time, we can make a more conscious decision, as for which product is better quality. This shall be our guideline if we would like to compare prices and if we are waiting for the sale of a certain product. If we are reading the cited webpages, it is worth making a categorization of the definitions, what we shall browse for. This way we can make the following topics interesting, not only in case of clothes, but in case of other products, such as food:

1. Conscious shopping: How to quit the bad habit of impulse shopping and to become a conscious consumer, what is the psychological background of being a shopaholic, how to get rid of it?

2. Advertisement: Who is it good for? Is the product capable of providing the advantage that is advertised?

3. Sales: Which are the basic sales techniques in supermarkets that make us buy the products offered for sale?

4. Promotions and discounts: Is the product really at a good price or is it just an incentive? Is it worth for the retailer or supermarket

to sell the product for a discount price? Is it really worth collecting points or is it just a simple marketing tool?

5. Reliability: Is the company behind the web shop a reliable one? Do they deliver on time or they just make a promise? How do they handle complaints?

6. Vote: You should not forget that your shopping choice is a vote, a decision. You should not support companies that make children work, carry out animal experiments and which did not switch to sustainable, chemical-free or minimum waste technologies.

7. Waste accumulation: If you are not using something you should give these items for charity as a donation, for those who need it or swap for items we need. You shall never throw anything to the garbage bin! You should enquire where these companies are! You should recycle everything, transform them and repair the things that don't work!

8. Bank loan costs: If you buy something with the help of a loan, you should obtain the relevant information from several banks, enquire about the loan conditions, should not immediately opt for the bank advertised in the supermarket! In general you should get information about the products of other banks, see whether they have a better choice, if yes, you should change banks.

9. If possible, use cash when shopping even if it is not comfortable. In this case the bank cannot charge you any costs unlike if you are using credit cards.

10. 30 miles: Obtain information, browse on internet for food that you can obtain at a lower price locally, from retailers located within 30 miles, not in supermarkets. Pay in cash rather than by bank card.

11. Season: Buy seasonal, locally produced, fresher and healthier vegetables and fruits rather than those offered by supermarkets! They are better than the ones that travelled a long way before arriving to supermarkets, not to mention storage time.

12. Do not buy tools which you already have or whose functions are already fulfilled by another tool! New tools seem to support your life, however if we have already bought and tried them, they prove to be no better than the traditional ones. Thus, they become nothing else but waste.

Kitchen tools

According to our experience, the items listed in point 12 are kitchen equipment. We can laugh about them when seeing a video or some photos, but this is the bloody reality. We would not manufacture these items if there was nobody to buy them. The example of Kevin Harrington[198] demonstrates how we can get rich from items that we buy and use once or on some occasions later on, now the same applies to kitchen tools. It is, of course, very subjective who likes which tool or appliance and how many times they get to use the items about which BuzzFeed[199] published a tremendous list. What shall be considered, do we need the tool or not? If the consumer tries any of these products only on a few occasions and no more, it is doubtless that the tool will become junk, no more but simple waste. Of course, at this time you already paid for it, thus the only option you have is to think well before purchasing: do we really need that tool or not. Everyone can decide where to draw the line, what to buy and what not.

However, we should not swing to the other extreme, either. We can buy a toaster, but we can also toast our bread in the oven if we apply the required technology. If we perch through the bread at three spots with a needle, we can toast it in any baking pans in such a way that it does not get burnt. However, if we do not have enough time, it is not worth the toil. Nevertheless, baking our own bread is a really good thing. It is worth making our own bread if we mold it, make it rise and bake it ourselves, it is fresh and very delicious and we have high expectations when it comes to organic bread and we have sufficient time for it during the weekend. It is not at all sure that buying a bread baking machine for this purpose where you just have to add the ingredients is worth trying. Especially if the bread made in that machine does not come up to the expectations. This is how we ended up, my mother bought a bread baking machine 20 years ago, which has almost become a junk by now. We wanted to use it, but we gave it up after five attempts, it only produced a bread of appropriate quality only twice in spite of the fact that we followed the instructions on the recipe during preparation and there were no changes in the basic ingredients, either. We should not forget that if we spend too much time on baking bread and baking does not bring the expected result, not only the basic ingredients were wasted, but time as well.

Wasting is a huge problem in the world

Wasting and accumulating waste in welfare societies is an immense problem in the world, and there are some data and figures related to buying clothes, which make it tangible for everyone. The British spend 44 billion pounds for clothes each year[200], however, 30% of the clothes they do not wear in the first year. As a consequence, clothes worth 140 pounds end up as waste each year, while a significant proportion of items offered for charity are sold further. In the United States[200] we are facing a similar situation as in case of the UK, the Americans produce 10 million textile waste each year, thus increasing gigantic waste piles. In vain are there more and more outlet shops, selling in discount shops or charity activity towards the countries of Africa or Asia, the clothes that have become waste will end up in the garbage bin anyway. It might also happen that the manufacturers eliminate the stocks that they were unable to sell, although it could be given to the poor as donation. Some years ago a statement made by Abercrombie &Fitch, the company producing luxury clothing[201] caused a big scandal, they said that they would rather destroy their stocks instead of customers seeing their brand worn by the homeless.

Of course, it is not only the United Kingdom or the US who are facing the problem of wasting, other welfare states are also concerned. However, there are some examples which demonstrate how useless shopping can be limited with the application of state and local government tools or by our own decision, at the same time improving waste management and recycling practices. Hopefully there will be countries following the Swedish example[202], and other countries will adopt these measures, since the Scandinavian country would table two draft legislations at the same time. One of them envisages to decrease the extent of the VAT in case if clothes, shoes, even bikes and household appliances are repaired, while the other legislation is aimed at returning half of the reparation costs to the owner of the household appliance in the form of a tax refund, with the objective not to discard the machine, thus trying to make Swedish economy more sustainable.

This step is logical, since there are many household appliances and utensils which land in the rubbish bin for going wrong, at the same time the average consumer is not interested in repairing it, because it is much easier to order another one from a webs hop. There are some other examples as well, of course, which would facilitate the reuse of our everyday tools. In Vienna, the Company responsible for Public Hygiene[203] has recently opened a shop, where anyone can buy the items that their earlier owners discarded or handed over at the places designated for this purpose beside landfills. There are lots of objects here, such as bikes, intact and ready to be used, books, children's toys, countless clothes, dishes and bowls, in other words everything that is used in a household. It is enough to look at the photos of the shop to see which are the objects that the average consumers would like to get rid of, what sort of tools they buy perfectly unplanned, as we can see. We can learn a lot from these two European cities but not only from them: Brazil is a poorer country where Jaime Lerner[204], the mayor of Curitiba started to eliminate piles of wastes accumulating in the cities some years ago by giving bus tickets, food or books to the poor in exchange for collecting waste in containers and not throwing them into the river anywhere around in the environment. The program was successful, it could be extended to households in the form of organized selective waste management, thus by the beginning of the 90s already 70% of the households participated in selective waste collection, recycling two-thirds of the waste in a city of 1.7 million inhabitants.

In a Japanese village, in order to avoid the accumulation of waste, selective waste collection was almost developed to perfection and they managed to recycle every possible waste, in a rather peculiar way. In 2015, Kamikacu[205] demonstrated an 80% recycling indicator compared to the earlier figure of 55% in 2005. The creators of the Zero Waste Plan first convinced the residents of the importance of the program's feasibility, and then they set up the Zero Waste Center which selected the waste, classified it into 34 categories and recycled the vast majority after the residents took it to the center. Even a video[206] has been made about it, which shows the entire process of selection and that you can make almost anything of the recycled material, such as kimonos, bags and children's toys.

Japan gained reputation not only for Kamikacu. In the Country of the Rising Sun extreme minimalism[207] is gaining ground, according to which we only keep the amount of objects available in our home that we actually use. If we look at the one-bedroom apartment of Fumio Sasaki or of any other minimalists, we not only realize the small living space, but also that there are hardly any objects around, thus they have a spacious, sunny room, just like in Bea Jonhson's house. Marie Kondo[208] wrote a book[209] about minimalism, which can be a starting point for those involved in waste reduction and how to change to a minimalist lifestyle.

You might remember that state funding in Japan promotes and encourages the fast construction of charging stations for electric cars. Although it might be considered as a question related to energetics, it has an impact on waste management, environment protection and sustainability and healthcare. A part of the Japanese people travel by train and metro all around the country, however, the emissions of fuel and diesel operated cars have to be taken into account, which might be suppressed in the country during the years to come due to governmental measures. If there is less waste getting in the air, it is not only the air that is improved, but people can stay healthier, since smog provokes several diseases. This favorable process could not have been launched without state funding, thus the Japanese government not only regulated the market, but they took some measures which do good to the environment and the welfare of the people living there due to the fact that there is no emission, that is, waste. There is less available money to be invested into treating illnesses due to emissions and for financing of medicines in health-care, and although the state is funding car purchase, this mentality can create a win-win situation.

Reusing and recycling

Years ago, a coffee bar opened in the Netherlands, where anybody could repair their broken toaster, scale-coated iron, or shoes about to losing the sole using the help of volunteers, or simply doing the job alone. The idea of Repair Cafe[210] was raised by Martine Postma, who wanted to do something for environmental protection and sustain-ability in her own way. The concept of repairing instead of immedi-ately throwing something to waste has soon widened into a campaign. In the Netherlands, a dozens of coffee bars are in place, but you can find several such places in lots of countries of the world including Germany, UK, France, Australia or even the US.

This example can be a precedent for anyone for many reasons. First, one does not need to garbage all the repairable and still usable tools, but then again, it draws the attention to conscious purchas-es, stating that you shall only buy a product which is not produced with planned obsolescence, planned life expectancy, which means that you can assume the product will be usable for many years with-out a problem. We'll see, it won't work for many brands, but we will buy more from the ones that do. The real objective is, however, like we saw in the minimalist example, to buy - or if we have already bought to keep - only the items absolutely necessary for our way of life. Unnecessary stuff can either be sold or traded, like we saw in the example of Laura – make the choice that fits you. Usable stuff shall be either used or recycled.

Countless articles and blog posts can be found on the internet presenting the recycling of specific gadgets. Just think of PET bottles or coke cans, thousands of great ideas were published on how to make use of them. Some of these ideas are really sweet, but with the mentality of a conscious shopper you do not need these gadgets as much as you do not need the original contents of the bottles. Clean water can be produced using a water cleaning device from tap water; coke can be harmful to health – why shall we buy anyway? Of course, anybody can decide where to set the limits, what to buy or not, since the best guiding principle is the same here, too: the best waste is the waste never created. More specifically, it shall not be created, because we don't wish to recycle it.

Let's see some examples from our own practice! After a while, my companion became tired of having to wash and store the probiotic yoghurt cans brought in by a small local company, since she thought that about 100 of them would be enough to raise the spring seedlings, so the additional cans could be garbaged. I told her, however, that every single spring there is a beginner showing up on one of the

Facebook sites dealing with self-sufficiency farming expecting the help of others, not having any cans but still wanting to do some gardening. Everybody's gonna benefit from taking the cans from us: the farmer not having to buy cans at special stores, and us, who managed to get rid of the unnecessary stuff. At the same time, our partner might also help us in the future, for example sending us seeds that could do the trick, bringing a better yield for us. Of course, we can also be questioned about why we produce litter instead buying the cans at the local market in a glass bottle. The company that delivers a fine tasting yoghurt to the smaller shops, yoghurt with a much better taste than the competitors' products, with a bit better price, too, unfortunately does not sell goods at the market. Therefore we cannot buy the product there locally, and as long as this is the situation, we are forced to produce waste that we could make use of. However, we do not buy pre-packed, sliced cheese from this company anymore, since plastic wrapper cannot be reused in any way. Instead, we buy cheese at the market made by a primary producer, who puts it right into our box. The primary producer would wrap the cheese into a paper bag labelled with his logo and contact number which we could burn during winter time, but we do not need it: the box is sufficient. And the reason why? You will find out soon.

We haven't yet decided whether to replace our "inherited" English toilet with a bidet or not, rendering the use of toilet paper unnecessary. So until we make a decision about buying the bidet, we are forced to produce litter, not only by the paper released into the environment, but also by the paper hoop that stays in our household. However, the hoops can have use: we slice them into many rings and pull them over unwanted wrapped adv. papers dropped in our mailbox. Therefore the hoop, together with the rings serve as fine firelighters, not having to use so many branches for the fire, but for the compost instead.

The examples above make it clear that a given object should always have a purpose in the household through its whole life cycle, otherwise it's already a waste, or is on the way to becoming one. It does not matter whether it's a piece of food packaging, clothing or kitchen tool. At the same time, the way we live our life producing waste and reusing it always serves as benchmark. We'll never be perfect, though and will always produce litter. But quantity makes a difference. So even if PET bottles can be used for watering in the garden[211] and aluminum cans can be cut into colorful butterfly decorations[212], it's up to you to decide whether you really need these things or not. We say not: if still, ask others to give you some of them after the contents are emptied; they would throw it to the waste anyway. We did the same thing the fall when we made deep-frozen grape juice, thus we estimated the need of 15 PET bottles of one liter per each. We asked the local innkeeper to give us these bottles and we'll do the same with the ½ liter beer cans with the purpose of making a beer collector, used as a solar water heater during the summer. Of course, we will need the 15 PET bottles next year at during harvest time, so now they are clean and waiting for their next life cycle.

Since when shall a given object be considered as waste, or unnecessary, unused stuff? Good question. You're the only one who knows the correct answer: there is no rule of thumb, because you should know whether you will ever need this object or not. However, because trying to balance is a part of life, it can be a guideline in our household as well. We get rid of something, other stuffs we keep. We buy something, and some not. Much easier with our eyes kept open…

Positive examples of saving money like a pro

You could read about a method published on US sites that could also be understood as a game[213], based on the concept of many a little makes a mickle. The game consisted of a method of saving a small amount of money every week and doubling it for a duration of 52 weeks. This way, we shall have a nice amount of money by the end of the year, spent on Christmas presents or anything else. It's important to start the game with a few bucks only, otherwise the savings could end in a crash, and you can start it all over again in January. This way of sparing is exceptionally suitable for understanding the purpose of economizing, since as we mentioned in connection with clothing, many consumers are simply unable to handle money, they do not know how to save and live from month to month.

Still, if one would save consciously, not only putting the stock aside but investing it as well, could make much more money. An Australian man[214] did exactly the same thing when putting aside a part of his salary of 10 dollars per hour earned as a pizza boy for a decade, bought run-down estates, then renovated and leased them. The philosophy of Tony Fleming is simple, yet extremely effective. In a press release he shared his secret: if one has an aim to invest into something, at the same time not spending money for unnecessary stuff such as parties and expensive travels, the remainder can be invested properly. It is really worth the trial, since by the age of 30 Fleming collected a fortune enough to start his pension savings. Despite of the hard work, he trained himself to establish his own company, investing in even more estates.

There are some people who cut down on costs in a different way, for example expenditures of the household. After his parents divorced, Jordon Cox[215] was responsible for handling the family's assets; he realized at the age of 13 that weekly expenditures can be reduced from 120 pounds to 10 by collecting vouchers and using them properly. However, the young man's success not only lies in decreasing household costs. He discovered other areas of cost saving methods as well, for example in connection with traveling. One day he wanted to travel from Sheffield to London, but instead of going by train, he opted for flying because it was worth it. The truth is, he had to touch Berlin and participate in a sightseeing tour, but the voucher guy – as his companions called him – did not care about it or about the fact that the trip took 13 hours longer this way. All that mattered to him was spending 44.07 pounds instead of 51.79. Over the past years, the young guy mastered his voucher-collecting method, he even kept seminars about how to economize and make a living with scarce income.

A young girl aged 21 hit the news in 2014 by eating better food and gathering more money and all the while producing no waste at all, even banishing the dustbin from her household. Lauren Singer[216], besides studying environmental protection at a New York University, one day made up her mind to give up collecting waste since she found studying environmental protection and scattering waste all around the planet quite controversial. It took her one year to switch to her new lifestyle but still, she learned not to throw anything into the dustbin. After graduating from university, Lauren summarized all the experience she gathered and started a new business[217] distributing the products she made herself. She achieved all this without producing waste, of course. She shares the knowledge by her blog[218] and videos[219] with those interested in her activity and her business is thriving.

What constitutes a waste for the majority of people seemed a tradeable and valuable product for Dan Cluderay from Worksop, England.

Thus, he specialized in buying cut-priced products just before their expiry date, mainly food from supermarkets and selling them at a higher price still lower compared to those of the supermarkets. As Cluderay has it, both the buyer and the seller gain with the method, since British housewives could make a 60 pound-save per week upon buying the products from him instead of going to the supermarket. Eventually, the supermarket profited as well, since the products that would be wasted, otherwise are sold at a low price before expiration. The astute man's company called Approved Food operates a website[220] that lets you browse cheap products at any time, they are available on Facebook[221] as well, reaching hundreds or even a thousand shares. The business has been thriving for years, since house-wives can make a 70 percent save per month when purchasing the food at Cluderay.

Positive examples can prompt us to integrate some of these good ideas into our daily routine even if we are not as professionals as the people above. At the beginning of our relationship, my partner used to bring the leftovers from her workplace that she bought in a buffet near her workplace, because she didn't want to waste it. Naturally, it seemed to be the right decision but it wasn't. After a short conversation I discovered the reason: the portions are big, and neither her, nor her colleagues can eat it. I suggested to her to form pairs and try to eat one portion including soup and a main dish: let's see if they are still hungry! A few days later it turned out that they weren't, so the advice became a practice, eliminating the need to take home the disposable food box several times a week. At the same time, instead of the estimated daily 6 dollars' lunch expenditure, bank executives had to pay only half of this price. Of course, some food was left sometimes, but it wasn't wasted or taken home: instead, an ambitious colleague committed to this task got the job of eating the leftovers, admitting that everything lands in our stomach eventually – causing quite a big delight with this striking solution. This latter solution wasn't my idea, of course, but my partner and her colleagues invented it: they found out how to develop this system. As a result of his commitment, this nice colleague was even relieved from paying the daily 3 dollars in many cases. After the colleagues have realized that my partner brings home-made meal several times a week to her workplace, they began to follow her example, thus cutting down on lunch costs. It is a simple calculation: if we assume that there are 20 working days in a month, it is easy to calculate that my partner spent 120 dollars on her daily meals per month in the beginning, producing of course a considerable amount of waste. When she started buying meals in pair with her colleague, this sum decreased to 60 dollars, but ever since she has been taking meals from home the calculation dropped to about 20-30 dollars. Maybe one day, when most of our food-stock is earned by self-sufficient production from winter till summer, this sum will take only a few bucks. By the way, my suggestion reached a fertile soil like a small seed: bank executives have quickly established a clear vision about how to handle waste and money spent on catering. It didn't cause them any problem since by means of their job, they know far too well how to handle money, and economize. Naturally it's no accident that the daily 60 dollars was not spent on everyday goods like clothing or shoes but just like Tony Fleming did, it was invested. Not into real estates but into bonds after collecting a bigger sum together with other savings.

Within years, cutting the costs could result in a reasonable fortune collected on our bank account which might contribute to our pension savings. Moreover, if you economize like Fleming did, you won't even have to wait but become a pensioner at the age of 30.

We wouldn't give you advices on finance, however, since this book was not written about this. Although there are many interesting statements in some bestsellers, school books or articles[222], which could be integrated in our mentality if we wanted to bring about an economizing way of life, we wouldn't recommend any books. Anyone with a deeper interest in the topic, you can find tons of literature on the internet.

If you have less waste and more money on your bank account as a result of reading this book, we'll be satisfied.

NOTES

1. http://www.cearchitects.com/green/

2. https://fa.financialavenue.org/how-much-will-a-well-insulated-house-save-you/

3. https://www.youtube.com/watch?v=fbRi8XROncM

4. https://www.youtube.com/watch?v=fbRi8XROncM

5. http://www.un.org/en/development/desa/news/population/world-urbanization-prospects-2014.html

6. http://www.ecowatch.com/revolutionary-family-shows-true-meaning-of-self-reliance-1882002295.html

7. https://www.mercer.com.au/newsroom/australia-could-become-regional-talent-hub.html

8. http://www.imdb.com/title/tt5545966/?ref_=ttep_ep3

9. http://risorse.legambiente.it/docs/tutti_in_classe_A_2.0000002287.pdf

*10. http://www.sciencealert.com/
here-s-why-trees-should-be-an-essential-part-of-urban-living-according-to-nasa*

11. http://www.nyc.gov/html/gbee/html/incentives/roof.shtml

12. http://www.brooklyngrangefarm.com/

13. https://www.nrdc.org/sites/default/files/GreenRoofsReport.pdf (page 12)

14. https://www.amazon.com/Big-Tiny-BuiltMyself-Memoir/dp/0399166173

15. http://www.dailymail.co.uk/news/article-3161760/Living-large-130-square-feet-Couple-sell-North-Carolina-mansion-travel-country-tiny-self-built-trailer-home.html

16. http://www.tinyhouseexpedition.com/

17. http://www.tinyhouseexpedition.com/blog/

18. http://www.tinyhouseexpedition.com/radio/

19. http://inhabitat.com/luxurious-tiny-home-lets-owner-live-off-grid-and-rent-free/

20. http://edition.cnn.com/2014/09/25/living/ecofriendly-shipwards-in-malmo/

21. https://www.fastcompany.com/3060167/this-new-neighborhood-will-grow-its-own-food-power-itself-and-handle-its-own-waste/1?show_rev_content

22. https://www.fastcoexist.com/3060167/this-new-neighborhood-will-grow-its-own-food-power-itself-and-handle-its-own-waste

23. http://urbanhomestead.org/

24. http://news.mit.edu/2016/hot-new-solar-cell-0523

25. https://smartenergyshow.wordpress.com/2011/03/18/a-new-source-of-energy-harnessing-ourselves/

26. https://www.youtube.com/watch?v=g8AtH7GR-JI

27. http://edition.cnn.com/2009/TECH/04/09/solar.oven.global.warming/index.html

28. https://www.expertise.com/green/lighting-efficiency-guide

29. http://www.huffingtonpost.com/2015/01/25/toilet-finder-app_n_6518116.html

30. http://www.comportone.com/cpo/landlord/articles/rellis/laundry.htm

31. http://www.bbc.com/capital/story/20150429-eat-with-strangers-make-money

32. http://toogoodtogo.co.uk/

33. https://www.iea.org/publications/freepublications/publication/MoreData_LessEnergy.pdf

34. https://homeadore.com/2016/07/19/tiny-apartment-kiev-art-studio/

35. https://www.dezeen.com/2016/07/12/yves-behar-fuseproject-mit-media-lab-ori-robotic-furniture-system-reconfigures-tiny-apartments/

36. https://www.eia.gov/electricity/data/browser/#/topic/7?agg=2,0,1&geo=g&freq=M

37. https://phys.org/news/2015-12-costa-rica-renewable-energy.html

38. https://www.youtube.com/watch?v=OctbJews2hc

39. https://www.welt.de/wirtschaft/article157308299/In-Deutschland-dreht-sich-der-Wind-gegen-die-Windkraft.html

40. http://www.reuters.com/article/us-rockefeller-exxon-mobil-investments-idUSKCN0WP266

41. https://www.santandercb.co.uk/knowledge-hub/un-2015-record-year-global-renewables-investment

42. http://www.pbs.org/newshour/bb/vermont-city-come-rely-100-percent-renewable-energy/

43. https://www.wien.gv.at/umwelt-klimaschutz/solarkraft-schoepfwerk.html

44. https://www.b2match.eu/energycall2016/participants/385

45. https://www.cnet.com/how-to/five-things-to-consider-before-buying-led-bulbs/

46. http://www.seriouseats.com/2010/05/how-to-cook-pasta-salt-water-boiling-tips-the-food-lab.html

47. Renewable sources — geothermal and hydropower — provide effectively all of Iceland's electricity and around 85% of the nation's total primary energy consumption, with most of the remainder consisting of imported oil products used in transportation and in the fishing fleet. Iceland expects to be energy-independent by 2050. Iceland's largest geothermal power plants are Hellisheiði and Nesjavellir, while Kárahnjúkar Hydropower Plant is the country's largest hydroelectric power station. When the Kárahnjúkavirkjun started operating, Iceland became the world's largest electricity producer per capita. - https://en.wikipedia.org/wiki/Iceland

48. http://www.huffingtonpost.com/2013/11/21/companies-responsible-for-global-warming_n_4316329.html

49. https://www.information.dk/udland/2013/01/kapitalisme-kritik-helt-ude-skoven

50. http://www.buildwithpropane.com/Propane-Systems/Furnaces-and-Boilers/Hybrid-Heating/

51. http://www.telegraph.co.uk/property/smart-living/draught-proofing-to-save-energy/

52. http://www.alamy.com/stock-photo-a-door-draft-excluder-in-the-shape-of-a-sheep-40075797.html

53. *https://www.youtube.com/watch?v=gCY9A599-oY and http://www.wickes.co.uk/ how-to-guides/home-maintenance/fit-draught-excluders*

54. *https://www.youtube.com/watch?v=zHj8Qxp3Bfk*

55. *https://www.fastcompany.com/3041322/hoffice-turns-your-apartment-into-a-free-and-incredibly-productive-coworking-space?show_rev_content*

56. *https://www.youtube.com/watch?v=KIoNUsCPgeg&t=28s*

57. *https://www.youtube.com/watch?v=kD6Vqj3ID6I*

58. *https://www.youtube.com/watch?v=fbRi8XROncM*

59. *https://www.usabreakingnews.net/2009/10/ does-jennifer-aniston-only-take-three-minute-showers/*

60. *http://www.sify.com/movies/why-cameron-diaz-doesnt-flush-her-toilet-news-hollywood-kkfrVAfefjasi.html*

61. *http://www.home-water-works.org/indoor-use/toilets*

62. *http://www.bbc.com/news/uk-england-norfolk-29552557?_ga=1.113905615.916690107 .1407856939*

63. *http://www.thesimpledollar.com/do-you-really-save-money-by-not-always-flushing/*

64. *http://www.thetinyhouse.net/composting-toilet-tips/*

65. *https://www.youtube.com/watch?v=u5VxGLXgwS8*

66. http://www.telegraph.co.uk/news/earth/agriculture/farming/6828878/Britain-facing-food-crisis-as-worlds-soil-vanishes-in-60-years.html

67. http://www.sciencenewsline.com/news/2016062716170038.html

68. https://www.youtube.com/watch?v=6N13ejCtxg0

69. https://www.youtube.com/watch?v=xRYAFSzI3HY

70. https://www.reference.com/beauty-fashion/many-people-don-t-shower-day-73a0f44b2943eb2b

71. http://www.betaboston.com/news/2015/07/07/bacteria-in-a-bottle-aobiome-offers-ways-to-stay-clean-without-traditional-soap/

72. www.motherdirt.com

73. http://www.twyfordbathrooms.com/tips/tipcategory/saving-water-in-the-bathroom/#gref

74. http://heavenlyhomemakers.com/how-do-you-clean-your-home-naturally-what-would-grandma-do

75. https://www.youtube.com/watch?v=KQfScRqyLB0

76. https://www.youtube.com/watch?v=vcCOruzFTgQ

77. http://www.modernsoapmaking.com/what-you-need-to-know-to-start-a-soap-business/

78. http://www.economist.com/news/obituary/21659686-burt-shavitz-co-founder-burts-bees-died-july-5th-aged-80-buzz-buzz

79. https://cleantheworld.org/about-us/

80. https://www.washingtonpost.com/news/to-your-health/wp/2016/09/02/fda-bans-some-antibacterial-soaps-and-body-washes/?postshare=5961472841263768&tid=ss_tw&utm_term=.063c2753e5a9

81. https://www.washingtonpost.com/news/to-your-health/wp/2016/09/02/fda-bans-some-antibacterial-soaps-and-body-washes/?postshare=5961472841263768&tid=ss_tw&utm_term=.58c379477809

82/A. http://www.nytimes.com/2007/07/10/science/10qna.html?_r=0

82/B. http://www.huffingtonpost.com/bill-chameides/chemical-marketplace-bar_b_2104678.html

83. http://www.huffingtonpost.com/2013/01/02/plastic-bottles-banned-concord-massachusetts_n_2395824.html?ncid=edlinkusaolp00000003

84. http://www.worldbank.org/en/topic/water/publication/high-and-dry-climate-change-water-and-the-economy?CID=WAT_TT_Water_EN_EXT

85. https://www.theguardian.com/commentisfree/2015/nov/29/climate-change-syria-civil-war-prince-charles

86. http://www.worldbank.org/en/topic/water/publication/high-and-dry-climate-change-water-and-the-economy?CID=WAT_TT_Water_EN_EXT

87. https://www.youtube.com/watch?v=bVzppWSIFU0

88. https://www.yourmechanic.com/article/the-most-and-least-expensive-cars-to-maintain-by-maddy-martin

89. http://www.popularmechanics.com/cars/a17175/most-googled-car-brands/

90. http://www.reuters.com/article/us-ford-autonomous-idUSKCN10R1G1

91. http://www.businessinsider.com/
report-10-million-self-driving-cars-will-be-on-the-road-by-2020-2015-5-6

92. https://www.tesla.com/blog/
all-tesla-cars-being-produced-now-have-full-self-driving-hardware

93. http://www.businessinsider.com/
elon-musk-tesla-autopilot-version-8-rolls-out-september-21-2016-9

94. https://www.engadget.com/2016/10/20/
tesla-wont-let-its-cars-autonomously-drive-for-uber-or-lyft/

95. https://www.nytimes.com/2016/10/26/technology/self-driving-trucks-first-mission-a-
beer-run.html?_r=0

96. http://www.copernicus.eu/news/98-big-cities-low-and-middle-income-countries-do-not-
meet-air-quality-standards

97. http://www.iflscience.com/environment/
air-pollution-kills-more-three-million-people-year/

98. http://europe.autonews.com/article/20150424/ANE/150409886/
plug-ins-poised-to-be-europes-top-electrified-drivetrain

99. http://www.autocarpro.in/news-international/
toyota-motor-europe-track-sell-300-hybrids-2016-21936

100. https://www.washingtonpost.com/news/wonk/wp/2013/04/22/why-arent-younger-
americans-driving-anymore/?utm_term=.a3d91672c525

101. https://en.wikipedia.org/wiki/Carsharing

102. http://www.demilked.com/chatillon-car-graveyard-abandoned-cars-vehicle-cemetery/

103. http://www.sciencedirect.com/science/article/pii/S0921800915000907

104. http://www.portfolio.hu/ingatlan/varos/budapesten_marpedig_jo_a_kozlekedes.236799.
html

105. http://www.independent.co.uk/life-style/gadgets-and-tech/news/commuting-online-
calculator-time-money-spend-travel-a6906721.html

106. https://www.kickstarter.com/projects/1266381423/
geoorbital-wheel-make-your-bike-electric-in-60-sec

107. https://www.youtube.com/watch?v=9BMcks55vfE

108. http://www.reliabilityindex.com/top-100

109. http://www.spiegel.de/auto/aktuell/dekra-report-2016-das-sind-die-besten-
gebrauchtwagen-a-1076938.html

110. http://www.huffingtonpost.co.uk/entry/
airbus-to-build-a-driverless-flying-taxi_uk_57bab295e4b0f78b2b4a869f

111. http://diversifynevada.com/news/news-articles/
historic-agreement-signed-between-goed-nias-ehang-to-advance-uas-research-d

112. https://www.youtube.com/watch?v=W1GfPwOpBYI

113. https://www.bloomberg.com/news/articles/2016-05-02/
gas-delivery-startups-want-to-fill-up-your-car-anywhere-is-that-allowed

*114. https://www.theguardian.com/world/2016/may/10/
japan-electric-car-charge-points-petrol-stations*

115. https://en.wikipedia.org/wiki/Hyperloop

*116. http://www.dailymail.co.uk/sciencetech/article-3915822/Dubai-Hyperloop-One-study-
potential-Abu-Dhabi-line.html*

*117. http://www.dailymail.co.uk/sciencetech/article-3915822/Dubai-Hyperloop-One-study-
potential-Abu-Dhabi-line.html*

118. https://www.youtube.com/watch?v=LeLAidJl5aw

119. https://www.youtube.com/watch?v=iKhsPO6yYko

120. http://www.theverge.com/2016/11/1/13487382/maglev-train-china-crrc-speed-record

121. http://fortune.com/2016/06/18/google-waze-difficult-intersection/

122. http://www.carscoops.com/2015/10/volvo-focuses-on-water-conservation.html

123. https://www.youtube.com/watch?v=q9bDLTTHId0

124. http://www.ascr.at/en/

*125. Róbert Baranyi lives with his girlfriend in Hungary a small country in Europe. They
live in a nice detached house with a garden in a village called Bocskaikert, close to the
country's second biggest city, Debrecen. They moved out of Debrecen in 2016, when they
completely gave up their city lifestyle. Today they both work, Robert is a lawyer and his
girlfriend works in a bank. The village where they live allows developing a self-sufficient
lifestyle, living in an economizing way, while producing minimal waste.*

126. https://www.fastcompany.com/3046277/
the-top-jobs-in-10-years-might-not-be-what-you-expect

127. http://timharford.com/books/adapt/

128. http://urbanhomestead.org/

129. https://www.youtube.com/watch?v=8r0CiLBM1o8

130. https://en.wikipedia.org/wiki/Community-supported_agriculture

131. https://www.facebook.com/GrowFoodNotLawns/?fref=ts

132. http://www.colomboherald.com/earth/cuba%E2%80%99s-organic-revolution

133. http://gyartastrend.hu/cikk/2030_ra_az_emberiseg_lehuzhatja_a_rolot

134. https://www.ted.com/talks/
stephen_ritz_a_teacher_growing_green_in_the_south_bronx#t-85672

135. http://www.pbs.org/newshour/bb/
one-college-turns-football-field-farm-sees-students-transform/

136. http://www.pbs.org/newshour/bb/
one-college-turns-football-field-farm-sees-students-transform/

137. http://rsfsocialfinance.org/2016/01/07/
bushwicks-black-brown-youth-enriched-by-composting-project/

138. https://www.ted.com/talks/jamie_oliver

139. https://simple.wikipedia.org/wiki/Overweight

140. https://www.eurekalert.org/pub_releases/2016-07/tl-tlo071216.php

141. http://www.dailymail.co.uk/femail/article-3792620/Mum-three-halves-weekly-food-bill-ditching-supermarket.html

142. https://www.foodpolicy.umn.edu/policy-summaries-and-analyses/food-loss-and-waste-us-science-behind-supply-chain

143. https://en.wikipedia.org/wiki/John_Yudkin

144. https://moly.hu/konyvek/menyhert-anna-szerk-kaloriakalauz

145. https://play.google.com/store/apps/details?id=ca.roncai.incentive&hl=en

146. http://www.dailymail.co.uk/femail/article-3873776/Obese-mother-gorged-peanut-butter-cuts-habit-loses-incredible-200lbs-realising-consuming-4-000-calories-DAY.html

147. https://www.kickstarter.com/projects/747005876/welt-the-smart-belt-for-fashion-and-health

148. http://www.calculator.net/calorie-calculator.html

149. http://www.businessinsider.com/supermarkets-make-you-spend-money-2011-7?op=1#ixzz2GSF7h1lX

150. http://theconversation.com/how-we-get-sucked-in-by-junk-food-specials-in-supermarkets-66392

151. http://www.fao.org/save-food/resources/keyfindings/en/

152. https://en.wikipedia.org/wiki/Wa$ted!_(U.S._TV_series)

153. http://www.huffingtonpost.com/entry/
rob-greenfield-wearing-trash-30-days-trash-me_us_57e98b63e4b0c2407cd8ab12

154. https://www.youtube.com/watch?v=0P1xEiPzShQ

155. http://rockdustlocal.com/uploads/3/4/3/4/34349856/americas_vanishing_nutrients.pdf

156. https://www.thelocal.fr/20160701/
what-does-frances-ban-on-plastic-bags-actually-mean

157. https://www.washingtonpost.com/news/worldviews/wp/2016/09/19/
france-bans-plastic-plates-and-cutlery/?utm_term=.0b8d08c9d90d

158. https://www.theguardian.com/environment/2016/jul/30/
england-plastic-bag-usage-drops-85-per-cent-since-5p-charged-introduced

159. https://www.sciencedaily.com/releases/2016/08/160821093046.htm

160. https://en.wikipedia.org/wiki/Zero_waste

161. http://www.zerowastehome.com/ - https://www.amazon.com/gp/product/B00A6CT012/
ref=as_li_qf_sp_asin_il_tl?ie=UTF8&tag=thez0d-20&camp=1789&creative=9325&link
Code=as2&creativeASIN=B00A6CT012&linkId=e71f8d4b15ba7f6d741aab51f37753bb -
https://www.youtube.com/user/ZeroWasteHome

162. http://bepakt.com/packaging-free-shops/ - http://original-unverpackt.de/ - http://
daybyday-shop.com/- https://in.gredients.com/

163. http://www.napi.hu/nemzetkozi_gazdasag/zsenialis_otlet_az_elhizas_ellen_
tudomanyos_szenzacio_az_uj_modszer.586379.html

164. http://www.nejm.org/doi/full/10.1056/NEJMc1602012#t=article–

165. http://repositorio.ispa.pt/bitstream/10400.12/3364/1/IJSP_998-1009.pdf

166. https://hu.wikipedia.org/wiki/L%C3%A1ng_Istv%C3%A1n_(agrok%C3%A9mikus)

167. http://www.pnas.org/content/111/46/16610.full

168. http://www.salon.com/2014/02/08/
the_creepy_crawly_solution_to_the_worlds_hunger_problems_eat_more_bugs/

169. http://luckypeach.com/baking-with-insect-flour/

170. https://www.nytimes.com/2014/01/08/dining/energy-bars-that-put-a-chirp-in-your-step.
html?_r=0

171. https://wellnessmama.com/

172. https://www.youtube.com/watch?v=iLep_SpvwKA

173. https://www.youtube.com/watch?v=qGfXLznJJY0&t=11s

174. http://www.economist.com/news/
obituary/21659686-burt-shavitz-co-founder-burts-bees-died-july-5th-aged-80-buzz-buzz

175. http://www.dailymail.co.uk/sciencetech/article-2316679/The-shirt-wear-100-DAYS-
washing-ironing.html

176. https://www.youtube.com/watch?v=Ap1-HW3vWc0

177. https://www.diynatural.com/homemade-cleaners/

178. http://www.ecologistnews.com/green-living/10-ultimate-tips-to-save-water-at-home.
html

179. http://www.ehow.com/how_7696461_wash-dishes-baking-soda-vinegar.html

180. https://www.amazon.co.uk/PERLATOR-PER143831-Perlator-Saving-Sprayer/dp/B008GC0O00

181. http://www.treehugger.com/green-home/faucet-attachment-reduces-water-use-98.html

182. https://www.diynatural.com/

183. https://www.amazon.com/Big-Tiny-BuiltMyself-Memoir/dp/0399166173

184. https://hassle.com/uk

185. http://www.huffingtonpost.com/2015/02/06/another-mother-business-stressed-out-students_n_6534412.html?utm_hp_ref=small-business&ir=Small+Business

186. https://www.youtube.com/watch?v=KQfScRqyLB0

187. http://www.lifehack.org/articles/lifestyle/extreme-minimalism-andrew-hyde-and-the-15-item-lifestyle.html

188. https://www.youtube.com/user/ZeroWasteHome

189. https://en.wikipedia.org/wiki/Kevin_Harrington_(entrepreneur)

190. http://www.harpersbazaar.com/culture/features/a10441/why-i-wear-the-same-thing-to-work-everday/

191. http://www.makingsenseofcents.com/2014/03/how-much-money-do-you-spend-on-clothing.html

192. http://www.huffingtonpost.com/mattias-wallander/closet-cast-offs-clogging_b_554400.html

193. https://www.fdic.gov/about/comein/files/foreclosure_statistics.pdf

194. http://www.huffingtonpost.com/2014/10/27/sarah-lazarovic-book-interview_n_6017260.html

195. https://www.forbes.com/sites/ryanmac/2016/04/21/the-realreal-continues-growth-raises-another-40-million/

196. http://www.mirror.co.uk/money/student-made-30000-selling-old-7424364

197. http://www.fcnb.ca/smart-buying-tips.html

198. https://en.wikipedia.org/wiki/Kevin_Harrington_(entrepreneur)

199. https://www.buzzfeed.com/laurenpaul/ridiculous-food-gadgets-you-definitely-need?utm_term=.gyaDDrY9L#.geoDDgnwx

200. http://www.bbc.com/news/magazine-30227025 and http://www.huffingtonpost.com/entry/clothing-donation-problem_us_57d85975e4b09d7a68803d90?7wr4o6mt3rtyjsjor

201. http://www.ecouterre.com/af-would-rather-trash-its-clothes-than-donate-them-to-the-homeless/

202. https://www.theguardian.com/world/2016/sep/19/waste-not-want-not-sweden-tax-breaks-repairs

203. https://48ertandler.wien.gv.at/site/

204. http://www.ted.com/talks/jaime_lerner_sings_of_the_city

205. https://www.theguardian.com/world/gallery/2008/aug/05/japan.
recycling?picture=336197909

206. https://www.youtube.com/watch?v=eym10GGidQU

207. http://www.reuters.com/article/us-japan-minimalism-idUSKCN0Z50VP

208. https://en.wikipedia.org/wiki/Marie_Kondo

209. http://tidyingup.com/

210. https://repaircafe.org/en/about/

211. http://www.providentliving.org.nz/bottle-drip-irrigation/

212. http://www.fabdiy.com/aluminum-can-butterflies/

213. http://lifehacker.com/take-the-52-week-money-challenge-and-easily-save-
about-1486564993

214. http://www.dailymail.co.uk/news/article-3832798/Sydney-investor-Tony-Fleming-owns-
14-properties-working-Domino-s-Pizza-ten-years.html

215. http://www.dailymail.co.uk/travel/travel_news/article-3419238/Teenager-saves-7-72-
train-journey-Sheffield-Essex-taking-PLANE-Berlin.html

216. http://www.mindbodygreen.com/0-16168/i-havent-made-any-trash-in-2-years-heres-
what-my-life-is-like.html

217. http://thesimplyco.com/

218. http://www.trashisfortossers.com/

219. https://www.youtube.com/channel/UCgjw6tZNyjR_8zIFDsIPpww

220. http://www.approvedfood.co.uk/

221. https://www.facebook.com/ApprovedFood

222. https://www.smallfootprintfamily.com/how-to-save-money-by-going-green

Contents

www.ingramcontent.com/pod-product-compliance
Lightning Source LLC
Chambersburg PA
CBHW071019280326
41935CB00011B/1411